THE PILGRIM'S PROGRESS

Published by Desiring God
Post Office Box 2901
Minneapolis, MN 55402
www.desiringGod.org

PERMISSIONS

Cover Design: Peter Voth

Typesetting: Ryan Leichty

TABLE OF CONTENTS

FOREWORD

Leland Ryken

The book that became known to posterity as *The Pilgrim's Progress* is a Christian classic whose importance is impossible to overstate. For more than two centuries after its first publication, *The Pilgrim's Progress* ranked just behind the King James Bible as the most important book in evangelical Protestant households. The book has been translated into some two hundred languages, including eighty in Africa. Any book that has achieved such popularity has a very large claim to our attention.

FACTS OF PUBLICATION

The Pilgrim's Progress actually has two publication dates, corresponding to the two books that comprise it. The first book was published in 1678 and bore the title *The Pilgrim's Progress: From This World to That Which Is to Come, Delivered Under the Similitude of a Dream.* It tells the story of the spiritual journey of the protagonist named Christian from the City of Destruction to the Celestial City (meaning heaven).

Book II was published six years later as part of an old artistic tradition known as a "companion piece." It tells the story of the same journey, this time undertaken by Christian's wife, Christiana, and their four sons. The two books continued to be published separately until 1728, not being published as a combined book until forty-four years after the first appearance of Book II. This new edition from Desiring God resembles the early publication strategy of *The Pilgrim's Progress* by releasing Book I individually.

Additionally, in order to provide more insight into the life of Bunyan, this new edition features an introduction by John Piper that traces the character of Bunyan's faith in the midst of suffering. This new edition also includes a preface written by John Newton in 1776. Newton's preface accompanied several publications of *The Pilgrim's Progress* in the eighteenth century, but has virtually been non-existent for the last century. The recovery of this preface and incorporation into the present volume sets it apart from other editions currently in print.

AUTHOR AND COMPOSITION

The author of *The Pilgrim's Progress* is John Bunyan (1628–1688), one of the most famous preachers in English history as well as a popular British author. Externally Bunyan led a difficult life. He was poor from childhood. He married his first wife at the age of twenty, and Bunyan once claimed that when the couple married they had not "so much household stuff as a dish or spoon betwixt us both." By Bunyan's own account, he led a wild youth and was converted at the approximate age of thirty.

Following his conversion, Bunyan felt a call to preach. Therein lay a difficulty. Religious tolerance had not yet arrived on the scene, and only one state-sanctioned Christian group enjoyed freedom of worship. In Bunyan's day that group was the Church of England, also known as the Anglican Church. Bunyan was a Baptist preacher who refused to stop preaching without an official license. As a result,

Bunyan found himself in and out of prison over a period of twelve years (1659–1671). While imprisoned, he eked out a living for his family by making shoe laces.

Much great literature and art have been produced in the crucible of suffering, and *The Pilgrim's Progress* is such a work. The consensus of scholarly opinion is that Bunyan wrote Book I of his masterpiece while in prison. (He is also reputed to have secretly carved a flute from a table leg in the prison.)

Bunyan was emphatically not a one-book author. Despite his chaotic and stressful external life (including the death of his first wife when he was approximately thirty and the blindness of his daughter Mary), Bunyan was a prolific author. He published over thirty books, mainly theological in nature.

Bunyan was also one of the most famous preachers of his day (which partly explains why the civil and Anglican officials singled him our for particularly harsh treatment). After his release from prison, Bunyan sometimes traveled all the way from his native Bedford to London to preach (a two-day journey in Bunyan's day). On one recorded event, 1,200 Londoners turned out on a cold winter morning to hear Bunyan preach.

Bunyan's death at the age of sixty was caused by pneumonia resulting from exposure to drenching rain while Bunyan made a two-day trip on horseback to heal relations between a father and his estranged son. Bunyan was buried in the famous nonconformist cemetery in London called Bunhill Fields. The monument on his tomb is today the most prominent site in the cemetery. On its side is the carved figure of a person carrying a burden on his back, a picture of the most famous moment in *The Pilgrim's Progress* where Christian loses his burden of sin at the foot of the cross.

THE PILGRIM'S PROGRESS AS A LITERARY CLASSIC

The Pilgrim's Progress is a paradox. On the one hand it is a work of folk literature. This makes it a book of the common people, just like the Bible. Through the ages, parents have read *The Pilgrim's Progress* to their children much as they read Bible stories to them. Reinforcing this identity of being a book for ordinary people rather than literary scholars is the religious nature of the book. It is a book of edification first, and beyond that it offers whatever entertainment value we might wish to find in it.

But that is only half of the picture. *The Pilgrim's Progress* is also a complex work of literature, appealing to people of literary sophistication as well as the common person. Perhaps no other literary masterpiece incorporates as many different literary genres as *The Pilgrim's Progress.*

The primary genre is narrative or story. This means that readers need to be ready to respond to the three narrative ingredients of setting, characters, and plot. Most storytellers excel in one of these or perhaps two, but we would be hard pressed to decide which of the three Bunyan is best at. He is good at all three. His ability to describe scenes cannot be surpassed. But just as we think that this is Bunyan's specialty, we remember his skill with character creation and remind ourselves that few authors have given us a greater gallery of memorable characters than Bunyan. And then we further recall that Bunyan's skill with plot is breathtaking.

What kind of story is The Pilgrim's Progress? The list of subgenres is nearly endless. The main storyline is a travel story, in the specific form of a perilous journey (surely one of the five greatest story motifs of all time). The virtues of the travel story are one of the leading appeals of The Pilgrim's Progress, as we are entranced by strange settings remote from our daily routine (though somehow familiar), encounters with unusual characters, and narrow escapes in abundance.

Many travel stories are quest stories, and this is true of *The Pilgrim's Progress*. The protagonists of the two books—Christian in Book I and Christiana in Book II—leave the City of Destruction in a search to find the Celestial City. The story of their quests is an adventure story par excellence. Danger and suspense greet us at every turn.

AN ALLEGORY

Much more could be said about the story qualities of *The Pilgrim's Progress*, but the really essential final thing that we need to note is that Bunyan's story is an allegory. An allegorical story is one in which the literal, physical level of action is intended as a picture of something else. Double meaning is at the heart of allegory. The details in an allegorical story stand for something else. In *The Pilgrim's Progress*, for example, a slough or bog (modeled, incidentally, on a notorious bog on the outskirts of Bunyan's home town) stands for spiritual despair over one's lost state.

There is a right way and wrong way to deal with the allegorical aspect of *The Pilgrim's Progress*. The wrong way is to slight the literal, physical level of action on the premise that the religious meaning is what really matters. The right way is to abandon ourselves to the story qualities of the work and let the second level of understanding grow out of that narrative experience. Giant Despair first of all needs to be a terrifying giant in our imagination, and *then* he becomes a picture of psychological and theological realities.

Allegory can easily become reductionistic, but this need not happen. For example, a character with the allegorical name of Talkative is immediately recognizable to us: he is someone who talks too much. But the Bunyan magic is such that Talkative is simultaneously (a) a personality type, (b) a social type (the overly talkative person who quickly becomes a social pest), and (c) a spiritual reality (someone who substitutes talk for genuine faith and Christian action). The allegorical names of Bunyan's characters should not lull us into thinking that they are one-dimensional.

THE RELIGIOUS VISION OF THE PILGRIM'S PROGRESS

Bunyan was a belated Puritan. Puritanism was the English branch of the Protestant Reformation. At every point in *The Pilgrim's Progress* we can see Puritan inclinations of mind and belief. The preoccupations of the book are Puritan—the Bible as the authority for religious belief (the book is a virtual mosaic of Bible verses); human sinfulness as the natural state of all people; salvation of one's soul as the one thing needful; the substitutionary atonement of Jesus as the basis for the forgiveness of sin; heaven as the ultimate longing of every person.

But the picture is a little more complex than simply calling Bunyan a Puritan. When Bunyan was finally freed from imprisonment, he became a Baptist preacher. If Bunyan were living today, we would call him an evangelical Christian, but more specifically a Reformed Calvinistic Baptist.

TIPS FOR READING BUNYAN'S MASTERPIECE

The Pilgrim's Progress is initially a difficult book for modern readers. The first obstacle is the archaic language of the book. The language of *The Pilgrim's Progress* is decidedly old-fashioned (like the King James Bible, which it more closely resembles than any other English-language literary work). The solution to the problem is to accept the archaic language as a feature of the book and enjoy it as part of its arresting strangeness (a phrase that comes from J.R.R. Tolkien's endorsement of fantasy and fairy tales as literary genres).

Secondly, the taste for allegory is today somewhat out of vogue (though it has always remained part of the folk imagination). We will fare just fine with Bunyan's allegorical story if we read it as a travel story and adventure story first, and then allow the theological and moral level to emerge as an extra source of enjoyment and edification.

Some people read *The Pilgrim's Progress* for edification and receive literary enjoyment as a byproduct. Others sit down to read it for its narrative qualities and gain edification as a byproduct. It makes absolutely no difference which of those two models is true for a given reader. What matters is that once we start to read the story we open ourselves to both aspects of the book—its literary qualities (which exist in abundance) and its religious meanings. *The Pilgrim's Progress* is a "crossover" book that appears in lists of both literary classics and religious (or even devotional) classics. It is an expansive book that holds up under virtually any approach that we bring to it. It is a book for all readers and all tastes.

TO LIVE UPON GOD WHO IS INVISIBLE

The Life of John Bunyan

BY JOHN PIPER

In 1672, about fifty miles northwest of London in Bedford, John Bunyan was released from twelve years of imprisonment. He was forty-four years old. Just before his release he updated his spiritual autobiography called *Grace Abounding to the Chief of Sinners*. He looked back over the hardships of the last twelve years and wrote about how he was enabled by God to survive and even flourish in the Bedford jail. One of his comments gives me the title for this short biography.

He quotes 2 Corinthians 1:9 where Paul says, "We had this sentence of death in ourselves, that we should not trust in ourselves, but in God that raiseth the dead." Bunyan writes,

> *By this scripture I was made to see that if ever I would suffer rightly, I must* first *pass a sentence of death upon every thing that can be properly called a thing of this life, even to reckon myself, my wife, my children, my health, my enjoyment, and all, as dead to me, and myself as dead to them. The* second *was,* to live upon God who is invisible, *as Paul said in another place; the way not to faint, is to "look not at the things which are seen, but at the things which are not seen; for the things which are seen are temporal, but the things which are not seen are eternal."*

The phrase that I have fastened on for the title, and focus of this study of Bunyan, is the phrase, "to live upon God who is invisible." He discovered that if we are to suffer rightly we must die not only to sin, but to the innocent and precious things of this world, including family and freedom.

We must "live upon God who is invisible." Everything else in the world we must count as dead to us and we to it. That was Bunyan's passion from the time of his conversion as a young married man to the day of his death when he was sixty years old.

SUFFERING: NORMAL AND ESSENTIAL

In all my reading of Bunyan, what has gripped me most is his suffering and how he responded to it—what it made of him, and what it might make of us. All of us come to our tasks with a history and many predispositions. I come to John Bunyan with a growing sense that suffering is a normal, useful, essential, and God-ordained element in Christian life and ministry—not only for the sake of weaning us off the world and teaching us to live on God, as 2 Corinthians 1:9 says, but also to make pastors who are more able to love the church (2 Tim 2:10; Col 1:24) and make missionaries who are more able to reach the nations (Matt 10:16–28), so that they can learn to live on God and not the bread that perishes (John 6:27).

I am influenced in the way I read Bunyan by both what I see in the world today and what I see in the Bible. As you read this book, there are sure to be flashpoints of suffering somewhere in the world. The followers of Jesus will suffer as long as the world stays and the word of Jesus stands. "In the world you have tribulation" (John 16:33). "Behold, I send you out as sheep in the midst of wolves" (Matt 10:16). Today churches are being burned in some countries, and Christians are being killed by anti-Christian mobs. Christians endure systematic starvation and enslavement. China perpetuates its official repression of religious freedom and lengthy imprisonments. India, with its one billion people and unparalleled diversity, heaves with tensions between major religions and extremist violence. There are consistent reports that thousands of Christians across the world die as martyrs every year.

And as I come to Bunyan's life and suffering, I see in the Bible that "through many tribulations we must enter the kingdom" (Acts 14:22); and the promise of Jesus, "If they persecuted me, they will also persecute you" (John 15:20); and the warning from Peter "not to be surprised at the fiery ordeal among you, which comes upon you for your testing, as though some strange thing were happening to you" (1 Pet 4:12); and the utter realism of Paul that we who "have the first fruits of the Spirit, even we ourselves groan within ourselves, waiting eagerly for *our* adoption as sons, the redemption of our body" (Rom 8:23); and the reminder that "our outer nature is wasting away" (2 Cor 4:16); and that the whole creation "was subjected to futility" (Rom 8:20).

As I look around me in the world and in the word of God, my own sense is that what we need from Bunyan right now is a glimpse into how he suffered and how he learned to "live on God that is invisible." I want that for myself, my family, and my church—and I want that for all who read this book. Nothing glorifies God more than when we maintain our stability and even our joy having lost everything but God (Hab 3:17–18). That day is coming for each of us, and we do well to get ready.

THE TIMES OF THE REDWOODS

John Bunyan was born in Elstow, about a mile south of Bedford, England on November 30, 1628, the same year that William Laud became the bishop of London during the reign of king Charles I. That connection with Bishop Laud is important because you can't understand the sufferings of

Bunyan apart from the religious and political times in which he lived.

In those days there were tremendous conflicts between Parliament and monarchy. Bishop Laud, together with Charles I, opposed the reforms of the Church of England desired by the Puritans. But in 1640, Oliver Cromwell—an advocate for the Puritans—was elected to Parliament, and civil war broke out in 1642 between the forces loyal to the king and those loyal to Parliament. In 1645, the Parliament took control of the Monarchy. Bishop Laud was executed that year and the use of the Book of Common Prayer was overthrown. The Westminster Assembly completed the Westminster Confession for the dominant Presbyterian church in 1646, and the king was beheaded in 1649. Cromwell led the new Commonwealth until his death in 1658. His main concern was a stable government with freedom of religion for Puritans, like John Bunyan and others, including Jews, who had been excluded from England since 1290 and finally allowed to return in 1655.

After Cromwell's death, his son Richard was unable to hold the government together. The longing for stability with a new king swelled (How quickly the favor of man can turn!). The Parliament turned against the Nonconformists like John Bunyan and passed a series of acts that resulted in increasing restrictions on the Puritan preachers. Charles II was brought home in what is known as the Restoration of the Monarchy, and proclaimed king in 1660, the same year that Bunyan was imprisoned for preaching without state approval.

TWO THOUSAND PASTORS EJECTED

In 1662, the Act of Uniformity was passed that required acceptance of the Prayer Book and Episcopal ordination. That

August, two thousand Puritan pastors were forced out of their churches. Twelve years later there was a happy turn of affairs with the Declaration of Religious Indulgence that resulted in Bunyan's freedom, his license to preach, and then his call as the official pastor of the non-conformist church in Bedford. But there was political instability until he died in 1688 at the age of 60. He was imprisoned one other time in the mid 1670's when he probably wrote *The Pilgrim's Progress*.

These were the days of John Bunyan's sufferings, and we must be careful not to overstate or understate the terror he experienced. We would overstate it if we thought he was tortured in the Bedford jail. In fact, some jailers let him out to see his family or make brief trips. But we would understate it if we thought he was not in frequent danger of execution. For example, in the Bloody Assizes of 1685, three hundred people were put to death in the western counties of England for doing no more than Bunyan did as a non-conformist pastor.

YOUNG HEARTACHE AND FEAR

Bunyan learned the trade of metalworking, also known as a "tinker" or "brasyer," from his father. He received the ordinary education of the poor to read and write, but nothing more. He had no formal higher education of any kind, which makes his writing and influence all the more astonishing. The more notable suffering of his life begins in his teens. In 1644, when he was fifteen, his mother and sister died within one month of each other. His sister was thirteen. To add to the heartache, his father remarried within a month. All this while, not many miles away in that same month of loss, the king attacked a church in Leighton and "began to cut and wound right and left." And later that fall, when Bunyan had turned sixteen, he was drafted into the Parliamentary Army. For about two years he was taken from his home for military service. There were harrowing moments he tells us, as once when a man took his place as a sentinel and was killed by a musket ball shot in the head.

Bunyan was not a believer during this time. He tells us, "I had few equals, especially considering my years, which were tender, for cursing, swearing, lying, and blaspheming the holy name of God . . . Until I came to the state of marriage, I was the very ringleader of all the youth that kept me company, in all manner of vice and ungodliness."

PRECIOUS BOOKS CAME WITH HIS WIFE

He "came to the state of matrimony" when he was twenty or twenty-one, but we never learn his first wife's name. What we do learn is that she was poor, but had a godly father who had died and left her two books that she brought to the marriage, *The Plain Man's Pathway to Heaven* and *The Practice of Piety*. Bunyan said, "In these two books I would sometimes read with her, wherein I also found some things that were somewhat pleasing to me; but all this while I met with no conviction." But the work of God's drawing him had begun.

John and his wife had four children: Mary, Elizabeth, John, and Thomas. Mary, the oldest, was born blind. This not only added to the tremendous burden of his heart in caring for Mary and the others, it would make his imprisonment when Mary was ten years old an agonizing separation.

"THY RIGHTEOUSNESS IS IN HEAVEN"

During the first five years of marriage, Bunyan was profoundly converted to Christ and to the baptistic, non-conformist church life in Bedford. He came under the influence of John Gifford, the pastor in Bedford, and moved from Elstow to Bedford with his family and joined the church there in 1653, though he was not as sure as they were that he was a Christian. It's hard to put a date on his conversion because in retelling the process in *Grace Abounding to the Chief of Sinners* he includes almost no dates or times. But we do know it was a lengthy and agonizing process.

He was pouring over the Scriptures but finding no peace or assurance. There were seasons of great doubt about the Scriptures and about his own soul. "A whole flood of blasphemies, both against God, Christ, and the Scriptures were poured upon my spirit, to my great confusion an astonishment . . . . How can you tell but that the Turks had as good scriptures to prove their Mahomet the Savior as we have to prove our Jesus?" "My heart was at times exceeding hard. If I would have given a thousand pounds for a tear, I could not shed one."

When he thought that he was established in the gospel there came a season of overwhelming darkness following a terrible temptation when he heard the words, "sell and part with this most blessed Christ . . . . Let him go if he will." He tells us that "I felt my heart freely consent thereto. Oh, the diligence of Satan; Oh, the desperateness of man's heart." For two years, he tells us, he was in the doom of damnation. "I feared that this wicked sin of mine might be that sin unpardonable." "Oh, no one knows the terrors of those days but myself." "I found it a hard work now to pray to God because despair was swallowing me up."

Then comes what seemed to be the decisive moment.

> *One day as I was passing into the field . . . this sentence fell upon my soul. Thy righteousness is in heaven. And methought, withal, I saw with the eyes of my soul Jesus Christ at God's right hand; there, I say, was my righteous-*

> *ness; so that wherever I was, or whatever I was doing, God could not say of me, he lacks my righteousness, for that was just before him. I also saw, moreover, that it was not my good frame of heart that made my righteousness better, nor yet my bad frame that made my righteousness worse, for my righteousness was Jesus Christ himself, "The same yesterday, today, and forever" (Heb 13:8). Now did my chains fall off my legs indeed. I was loosed from my afflictions and irons; my temptations also fled away; so that from that time those dreadful scriptures of God [about the unforgivable sin] left off to trouble me; now went I also home rejoicing for the grace and love of God.*

Under God, one key influence here, besides Pastor Gifford in Bedford, was Martin Luther. "The God in whose hands are all our days and ways, did cast into my hand one day a book of Martin Luther's; it was his *Commentary on Galatians* . . . . I found my condition in his experience so largely and profoundly handled, as if his book had been written out of my heart . . . . I do prefer this book of Martin Luther upon the Galatians, excepting the Holy Bible, before all the books that ever I have seen, as most fit for a wounded conscience."

A PREACHER IS BORN

So in 1655, when the matter of his soul was settled, he was asked to exhort the church, and suddenly a great preacher was discovered. He would not be licensed as a pastor of the Bedford church until seventeen years later, but his popularity as a powerful lay preacher exploded. The extent of his work grew. "When the country understood that the tinker had turned preacher," John Brown tells us, "they came to hear the word by hundreds, and that from all parts." Charles Doe, a comb maker in London, said (later in Bunyan's life),

"Mr. Bunyan preached so New Testament-like he made me admire and weep for joy, and give him my affections." In the days of toleration, a day's notice would get a crowd of over a thousand to hear him preach at seven o'clock in the morning on a weekday. Once, in prison, a whole congregation of sixty people were arrested and brought in at night. A witness tells us, "I . . . heard Mr. Bunyan both preach and pray with that mighty spirit of Faith and Plerophory of Divine Assistance, that . . . made me stand and wonder." The greatest Puritan theologian and contemporary of Bunyan, John Owen, when asked by King Charles why he, a great scholar, went to hear an uneducated tinker preach, replied, "I would willingly exchange my learning for the tinker's power of touching men's hearts."

THE INCREDIBLE ELIZABETH BUNYAN

In 1658, ten years after he was married, when Bunyan was thirty, his wife died, leaving him with four children under ten, one of them blind. A year later, he married Elizabeth, who was a remarkable woman. The year after their marriage, Bunyan was arrested and put in prison. She was pregnant with their firstborn and miscarried in the crisis. Then she cared for the Bunyan children as their step-mother for twelve years alone, and bore Bunyan two more children, Sarah and Joseph.

She deserves at least one story here about her valor in the way she went to the authorities in August of 1661, a year after John's imprisonment. She had already been to London with one petition. Now, as recounted by Bunyan's biographer, she was met with one stiff question:

"Would he stop preaching?"

"My lord, he dares not leave off preaching as long a he can speak."

"What is the need of talking?"

"There is need for this, my lord, for I have four small children that cannot help themselves, of which one is blind, and we have nothing to live upon but the charity of good people."

Matthew Hale with pity asks if she really has four children being so young.

"My lord, I am but mother-in-law to them, having not been married to him yet full two years. Indeed, I was with child when my husband was first apprehended; but being young and unaccustomed to such things, I being smayed at the news, fell into labor, and so continued for eight days, and then was delivered; but my child died."

Hale was moved, but other judges were hardened and spoke against him. "He is a mere tinker!"

"Yes, and because he is a tinker and a poor man, therefore he is despised and cannot have justice."

One Mr. Chester is enraged and says that Bunyan will preach and do as he wishes.

"He preacheth nothing but the word of God!" she says.

Mr. Twisden, in a rage: "He runneth up and down and doeth harm."

"No, my lord, it is not so; God hath owned him and done much good by him."

The angry man: "His doctrine is the doctrine of the devil."

She: "My lord, when the righteous Judge shall appear, it will be known that his doctrine is not the doctrine of the devil!"

Bunyan's biographer comments, "Elizabeth Bunyan was

simply an English peasant woman: could she have spoken with more dignity had she been a crowned queen?"

IMPRISONED FROM "MY POOR BLIND CHILD"

So for twelve years Bunyan chooses prison and a clear conscience over freedom and a conscience soiled by the agreement not to preach. He could have had his freedom when he wanted it. But he and Elizabeth were made of the same stuff. When asked to recant and not to preach he said,

> *If nothing will do unless I make of my conscience a continual butchery and slaughter-shop, unless, putting out my own eyes, I commit me to the blind to lead me, as I doubt not is desired by some, I have determined, the Almighty God being my help and shield, yet to suffer, if frail life might continue so long, even till the moss shall grow on mine eye-brows, rather than thus to violate my faith and principles.*

Nevertheless he was sometimes tormented that he may not be making the right decision in regard to his family.

> *The parting with my Wife and poor children hath often been to me in this place as the pulling of the Flesh from my bones; and that not only because I am somewhat too fond of these great Mercies, but also because I should have often brought to my mind the many hardships, miseries and wants that my poor Family was like to meet with should I be taken from them, especially my poor blind child, who lay nearer my heart than all I had besides; O the thoughts of the hardship I thought my Blind one might go under, would break my heart to pieces.*

PERSEVERING IN BEDFORD, NOT LONDON

Yet he stayed in Bedford. In 1672 he was released because of the Declaration of Religious Indulgence. Immediately he was licensed as the pastor of the church in Bedford, which he had been serving all along, even from within prison by writings and periodic visits. A barn was purchased and renovated as their first building and this is where Bunyan ministered as pastor for the next sixteen years until his death. He never was wooed away from this little parish by the larger opportunities in London. The estimate is that, in 1676, there were perhaps 120 non-conformists in Bedford, with others undoubtedly coming to hear him from around the surrounding villages.

There was one more imprisonment in the winter and spring of 1675–76. John Brown thinks that this was the time when *The Pilgrim's Progress* was written. But even though Bunyan wasn't in prison again during his ministry, the tension of the days was extraordinary. Ten years after his last imprisonment in the mid-1680's, persecution was heavy again. "Richard Baxter, though an old man now, was shut up in jail, where he remained for two years more, and where he had innumerable companions in distress."

Meetings were broken in upon, worshipers hurried to prison, "separatists changed the place of gathering from time to time, set their sentinels on the watch, left off singing hymns in their services, and for the sake of greater security worshipped again and again at the dead of night. Ministers were introduced to their pulpits through trap-doors in floor or ceiling, or through doorways extemporized in walls." Bunyan expected to be taken away again and deeded over all his possessions to his wife Elizabeth so that she would not be ruined by his fines or imprisonment.

A PILGRIM DIES AWAY FROM HOME

But God spared him, until August 1688. In that month he traveled the fifty miles to London to preach and to help make peace between a man in his church and his alienated father. He was successful in both missions. But after a trip to an outlying district, he returned to London on horseback through excessive rains. He fell sick of a violent fever, and on August 31, 1688, at age sixty, Bunyan followed his famous fictional Pilgrim from the "City of Destruction" across the river to the "New Jerusalem."

His last sermon had been on August 19 in London at Whitechapel on John 1:13. His last words from the pulpit were, "Live like the children of God, that you may look your Father in the face with comfort another day." His wife and children were probably unaware of the crisis till after it was too late. It is likely that Bunyan died without the comfort of family—just as he had spent so much of his life without the comforts of home. "The inventory of Bunyan's property after his death added up to a total of forty-two pounds and nineteen shillings. This is more than the average tinker would leave, but it suggests that most of the profits from *The Pilgrim's Progress* had gone to printers of pirated editions." He was born poor and never let himself become wealthy in this life. He is buried in London at Bunhill Fields.

So, in sum, we can include in Bunyan's sufferings the early, almost simultaneous, death of his mother and sister; the immediate remarriage of his father; the military draft in the midst of his teenage grief; the discovery that his first child was blind; the spiritual depression and darkness for the early years of his marriage; the death of his first wife leaving him with four small children; a twelve year imprisonment cutting him off from his family and church; the constant stress and uncertainty of imminent persecution, including one more imprisonment; and the final sickness and death far from those he loved most. And this summary doesn't include any of the normal pressures and pains of ministry and marriage and parenting and controversy and criticism and sickness along the way.

WRITING FOR THE AFFLICTED CHURCH

The question, then, that I bring to Bunyan's suffering is: What was its effect? How did he respond to it? What did it bring about? What difference did it make in his life? Knowing that I am leaving out many important things, I would answer that with five observations.

1. Bunyan's suffering confirmed him in his calling as a writer, especially for the afflicted church.

Probably the greatest distortion of Bunyan's life in the portrait I have given you so far is that it passes over one of the major labors of his life: his writing. Books had awakened his own spiritual quest and guided him in it. Books would be his main legacy to the church and the world.

Of course, he is famous for *The Pilgrim's Progress*—"next to the Bible, perhaps the world's best-selling book . . . translated into over 200 languages." It was immediately successful with three editions in the first year it was published in 1678. It was despised at first by the intellectual elite, but as Lord Macaulay points out, "*The Pilgrim's Progress* is perhaps the only book about which, after the lapse of a hundred years, the educated minority has come over to the opinion of the common people."

But most people don't know that Bunyan was a prolific writer before and after *The Pilgrim's Progress*. Christopher Hill's index of "Bunyan's Writings" lists fifty-eight books.

The variety in these books was remarkable: controversy (like those concerning the Quakers, and concerning justification and baptism), collections of poems, children's literature, allegory (like *The Holy War* and *The Life and Death of Mr. Badman*). But the vast majority were practical doctrinal expositions of Scripture built from sermons for the sake of strengthening and warning and helping Christian pilgrims make their way successfully to heaven.

He was a writer from beginning to end. He had written four books before he went to prison at age thirty-two, and in one year alone—1688, the year he died—five books were published. This is extraordinary for a man with no formal education. He knew neither Greek nor Hebrew, and had no theological degrees. This was such an offense even in his own day that his pastor, John Burton, came to his defense, writing a foreword for his first book in 1656 (when he was 28):

> *This man is not chosen out of an earthly but out of the heavenly university, the Church of Christ . . . . He hath through grace taken these three heavenly degrees, to wit, union with Christ, the anointing of the Spirit, and experiences of the temptations of Satan, which do more fit a man for that mighty work of preaching the Gospel than all university learning and degrees that can be had.*

Bunyan's suffering left its mark on all his written work. George Whitefield said of *The Pilgrim's Progress*, "It smells of the prison. It was written when the author was confined in Bedford jail. And ministers never write or preach so well as when under the cross: the Spirit of Christ and of Glory then rests upon them."

The fragrance of affliction was on most of what he wrote. In fact, I suspect that one of the reasons the Puritans are still being read today with so much profit is that their entire experience, unlike ours, was one of persecution and suffering. To our chipper age (at least in the prosperous West) this may seem somber at times, but the day you hear that you have cancer, or that your child is blind, or that a mob is coming, you turn away from the chipper books to the weighty ones that were written on the precipice of eternity where the fragrance of heaven and the stench of hell are both in the air.

Bunyan's writings were an extension of his pastoral ministry, mainly to his flock in Bedford who lived in constant danger of harassment and prison. His suffering fit him well for the task. Which leads to the second effect of Bunyan's suffering I want to mention.

2. Bunyan's suffering deepened his love for his flock and gave his pastoral labor the fragrance of eternity.

His writings were filled with love to his people. For example, three years into his imprisonment he wrote a book called *Christian Behavior*, which he ended like this:

> *Thus have I, in a few words, written to you before I die, a word to provoke you to faith and holiness, because I desire that you may have the life that is laid up for all them that believe in the Lord Jesus, and love one another, when I am deceased. Though then I shall rest from my labors, and be in paradise, as through grace I comfortably believe, yet it is not there, but here, I must do you good. Wherefore, I not knowing the shortness of my life, nor the hindrance that hereafter I may have of serving my God and you, I have taken this opportunity to present these few lines unto you for your edification.*

In his autobiography, written about halfway through his imprisonment, he spoke of his church and the effect he hoped his possible martyrdom would have on them: "I did often say before the Lord, that if to be hanged up presently before their eyes would be means to awake in them and confirm them in the truth, I gladly should consent to it." In fact, many of his flocked joined him in jail and he ministered to them there. He echoed the words of Paul when he described his longings for them: "In my preaching I have really been in pain, I have, as it were, travailed to bring forth Children to God."

He gloried in the privilege of the gospel ministry. This too flowed from his suffering. If all is well and this world is all that matters, a pastor may become jealous of prosperous people who spend their time in leisure. But if suffering abounds, and if prosperity is a cloak for the true condition of frisky, fun-loving perishing Americans, then being a pastor may be the most important and glorious of all work. Bunyan thought it was: "My heart hath been so wrapped up in the glory of this excellent work, that I counted myself more blessed and honored of God by this, than if I had made me the emperor of the Christian world, or the lord of all the glory of the earth without it."

He loved his people, he loved the work, and he stayed with it and with them to the end of his life. He served them and he served the world from a village parish with perhaps 120 members.

3. Bunyan's suffering opened his understanding to the truth that the Christian life is hard and that following Jesus means having the wind in your face.

In 1682, six years before his death, he wrote a book called *The Greatness of the Soul,* based on Mark 8:36–37, "What does it profit a man to gain the whole world, and forfeit his soul? For what will a man give in exchange for his soul?"

He says that his aim is to "awaken you, rouse you off of your beds of ease, security, and pleasure, and fetch you down upon your knees before him, to beg of him grace to be concerned about the salvation of your souls." And he does not mean the point of conversion but the process of perseverance. "The one who endures to the end, he will be saved" (Mark 13:13). He hears Jesus warning us that life with him is hard:

> *Following of me is not like following of some other masters. The wind sits always on my face and the foaming rage of the sea of this world, and the proud and lofty waves thereof do continually beat upon the sides of the bark or ship that myself, my cause, and my followers are in; he therefore that will not run hazards, and that is afraid to venture a drowning, let him not set foot into this vessel.*

Two years later, commenting on John 15:2 ("Every branch that bears fruit, he prunes"), he says, "It is the will of God, that they that go to heaven should go thither hardly or with difficulty. The righteous shall scarcely be saved. That is, they shall, but yet with great difficulty, that it may be the sweeter."

He had tasted this at the beginning of his Christian life and at every point along the way. In the beginning: "My soul was perplexed with unbelief, blasphemy, hardness of heart, questions about the being of God, Christ, the truth of the Word, and certainty of the world to come: I say, then I was greatly assaulted and tormented with atheism." "Of all the temptations that ever I met with in my life, to question the being of God and the truth of his gospel is the worst, and the worst to be borne."

In *The Excellency of a Broken Heart* (the last book he took to the publisher) he says,

> *Conversion is not the smooth, easy-going process some men seem to think . . . . It is wounding work, of course, this breaking of the hearts, but without wounding there is no saving. . . . Where there is grafting there is a cutting, the scion must be let in with a wound; to stick it on to the outside or to tie it on with a string would be of no use. Heart must be set to heart and back to back, or there will be no sap from root to branch, and this I say, must be done by a wound.*

Bunyan's suffering made him passionate about these things—and patient. You can hear his empathy with strugglers in these typically earthy words in a book from 1678 called *Come and Welcome to Jesus Christ*:

> *He that comes to Christ cannot, it is true, always get on as fast as he would. Poor coming soul, thou art like the man that would ride full gallop whose horse will hardly trot. Now the desire of his mind is not to be judged of by the slow pace of the dull jade he rides on, but by the hitching and kicking and spurring as he sits on his back. Thy flesh is like this dull jade, it will not gallop after Christ, it will be backward though thy soul and heaven lie at stake.*

It seems to me that Bunyan knew the balance of Philippians 2:12–13, "So then, my beloved . . . work out your salvation with fear and trembling; for it is God who is at work in you, both to will and to work for His good pleasure." First, he publishes a book called *Saved By Grace* based on Ephesians 2:5, "By grace you are saved." And then in the same year he follows it with a book called, *The Strait Gate*, based on Luke 13:24, "Strive to enter at the strait gate; for many, I say unto you, will seek to enter in, and shall not be able."

Bunyan's sufferings had taught him the words of Jesus

first hand, "The way is hard, that leads to life, and those who find it are few" (Matt. 7:14).

4. Bunyan's sufferings strengthened his assurance that God is sovereign over all the afflictions of his people and will bring them safely home.

There have always been, as there are today, people who try to solve the problem of suffering by denying the sovereignty of God—that is the all-ruling providence of God over Satan and over nature and over human hearts and deeds. But it is remarkable how many of those who stand by the doctrine of God's sovereignty over suffering have been those who suffered most and who found in the doctrine the most comfort and help.

Bunyan was among that number. In 1684 he wrote an exposition for his suffering people based on 1 Peter 4:19: "Let them that suffer according to the will of God commit the keeping of their souls to him in well doing, as unto a faithful Creator." The book was called *Seasonable Counsels: Advice to Sufferers*. He takes the phrase "according to the will of God," and unfolds the sovereignty of God in it for the comfort of his people.

> *It is not what enemies will, nor what they are resolved upon, but what God will, and what God appoints; that shall be done. . . . No enemy can bring suffering upon a man when the will of God is otherwise, so no man can save himself out of their hands when God will deliver him up for his glory. . . [just as Jesus showed Peter "by what death he would glorify God"]. We shall or shall not suffer, even as it pleaseth him.*

Thus God has appointed the persons who will suffer, the

time of their suffering, the place of their suffering, and how they will suffer.

"God has appointed who shall suffer"

In the first case, "God has appointed who shall suffer. Suffering comes not by chance, or by the will of man, but by the will and appointment of God." Thus Bunyan cites 1 Thessalonians 3:3 (KJV): ". . . that no man should be moved by these afflictions: for yourselves know that we are appointed thereunto." We must not think that suffering is a strange thing for those who fear God (1 Pet 4:12), he reminds us and appeals to Revelation 6:11 where the martyrs under the altar in heaven are told "that they should rest for a little while longer, until the number of their fellow servants and their brethren who were to be killed ["mark that," Bunyan says] even as they had been, would be completed also." An appointed number of martyrs! From which Bunyan concludes, "Suffering for righteousness and for righteousness' sake, is by the will of God. God has appointed who shall suffer."

"My Times Are in Thy Hands"

Secondly, God has appointed *when* they shall suffer . . . for his truth in the world. Suffering for such and such a man are timed, as to when he shall be tried for his faith." Hence when Paul was afraid in Corinth, the Lord strengthened him in a dream by saying, "Do not be afraid any longer, but go on speaking and do not be silent; for I am with you, and no man will attack you in order to harm you, for I have many people in this city" (Acts 18:9–10). "His time of suffering," Bunyan says, "was not yet come there." In the same way it was said of Jesus, "They sought to take him: but no man laid hands on him, because his hour was not yet come" (John

7:30, KJV). Bunyan concludes, "The times, then, and the seasons, even for the sufferings of the people of God, are not in the hands of their enemies, but in the hand of God; as David said, 'My times are in thy hand'" (Ps 31:15).

"By the Hand of God Here and There"

Thirdly, God has appointed *where* this, that, or the other good man shall suffer. Moses and Elias [Elijah], when they appeared on the holy mount, told Jesus of the suffering which he should accomplish at Jerusalem" (Luke 9:30–31). "The saints are sprinkled by the hand of God here and there, as salt is sprinkled upon meat to keep it from stinking. And as they are sprinkled, that they may season the earth; so accordingly, where they must suffer is also appointed for the better confirming of the truth. Christ said, it could not be that a prophet should 'perish out of Jerusalem' (Luke 13:33). But why . . . ? God has appointed that they should suffer there. So then, who, when, and where, is at the will of God, and they, accordingly, are ordered by that will."

"By What Death He Should Glorify God"

Fourth, "God has appointed . . . *what kind of sufferings* this or that saint shall undergo. . . . God said that he would show Paul beforehand how great things he should suffer for his sake (Acts 9:16). And it is said that Christ did signify to Peter beforehand 'by what death he should glorify God' (John 21:19)." As with the time and place and persons, so it is with the kind of sufferings we endure: They "are all writ down in God's book; and though the writing seem as unknown characters to us, yet God understands them very well. . . . It is appointed who of them should die of hunger, who with the sword, who should go into captivity, and who should be eating up of beasts. Let it then be concluded, that hitherto it appears, that the sufferings of saints are ordered and disposed by the will of God."

We could go even further with Bunyan as he shows "for what truth" his saints will suffer, and "by whose hand" and "how long." But let us ask, What is Bunyan's aim in this exposition of the sovereignty of God in suffering? He tells us plainly: "I have, in a few words, handled this . . . to show you that our sufferings are ordered and disposed by him, that you might always, when you come into trouble for this name, not stagger nor be at a loss, but be stayed, composed, and settled in your minds, and say, 'The will of the Lord be done.' (Acts 21:14)."

The Mercy That We Suffer Rather Than Torture

He warns against feelings of revenge.

> *Learn to pity and bewail the condition of the enemy . . . Never grudge them their present advantages. 'Fret not thy self because of evil men. Neither be thou envious at the workers of iniquity' (Prov. 24:19). Fret not, though they spoil thy resting place. It is God that hath bidden them do it, to try thy faith and patience thereby. Wish them no ill with what they get of thine; it is their wages for their work, and it will appear to them ere long that they have earned it dearly. . . . Bless God that thy lot did fall on the other side. . . . How kindly, therefore, doth God deal with us, when he chooses to afflict us but for a little, that with everlasting kindness he may have mercy upon us (Isa 54:7–8).*

"No Fruit, Because There Is no Winter There"

The key to suffering rightly is to see in all things the hand of a merciful and good and sovereign God and "to live upon God who is invisible." There is more of God to be had in times of suffering than any other time.

> *There is that of God to be seen in such a day as cannot be seen in another. His power in holding up some, his wrath in leaving of others; his making of shrubs to stand, and his suffering of cedars to fall; his infatuating of the counsels of men, and his making of the devil to outwit himself; his giving of his presence to his people, and his leaving of his foes in the dark; his discovering [disclosing] the uprightness of the hearts of his sanctified ones, and laying open the hypocrisy of others, is a working of spiritual wonders in the day of his wrath, and of the whirlwind and storm. . . . We are apt to overshoot, in the days that are calm, and to think ourselves far higher, and more strong than we find we be, when the trying day is upon us. . . . We could not live without such turnings of the hand of God upon us. We should be overgrown with flesh, if we had not our seasonable winters. It is said that in some countries trees will grow, but will bear no fruit, because there is no winter there.*

So Bunyan begs his people to humble themselves under the mighty hand of God and trust that all will be for their good. "Let me beg of thee, that thou wilt not be offended either with God, or men, if the cross is laid heavy upon thee. Not with God, for he doth nothing without a cause, nor with men, for . . . they are the servants of God to thee for good. (Ps 17:14 KJV; Jer 24:5). Take therefore what comes to thee from God by them, thankfully."

5. Bunyan's suffering deepened in him a confidence in the Bible as the word of God and a passion for biblical exposition as the key to perseverance.

If "living upon God who is invisible" is the key to suffering rightly, what is the key to living upon God? Bunyan's answer is to lay hold on Christ through the word of God, the Bible. Prison proved for Bunyan to be a hallowed place of communion with God because his suffering unlocked the word and the deepest fellowship with Christ he had ever known.

> *I never had in all my life so great an inlet into the Word of God as now [in prison]. Those scriptures that I saw nothing in before were made in this place and state to shine upon me. Jesus Christ also was never more real and apparent than now. Here I have seen him and felt him indeed. . . I have had sweet sights of the forgiveness of my sins in this place, and of my being with Jesus in another world. . . I have seen that here that I am persuaded I shall never, while in this world, be able to express.*

"In My Chest Pocket I Have a Key"

He especially cherished the promises of God as the key for opening the door of heaven.

> *I tell thee, friend, there are some promises that the Lord hath helped me to lay hold of Jesus Christ through and by, that I would not have out of the Bible for as much gold and silver as can lie between York and London piled up to the stars.*

One of the greatest scenes in *The Pilgrim's Progress* is when Christian recalls in the dungeon of Doubting-castle that he has a key to the door. Very significant is not only what the key is, but where it is:

> *"What a fool I have been, to lie like this in a stinking dungeon, when I could have just as well walked free. In my chest pocket I have a key called Promise that will, I am thoroughly persuaded, open any lock in Doubting-Castle." "Then," said Hopeful, "that is good news. My good brother, do immediately take it out of your chest pocket and try it." Then Christian took the key from his chest and began to try the lock of the dungeon door; and as he turned the key, the bolt unlocked and the door flew open with ease, so that Christian and hopeful immediately came out.*

"Prick Him Anywhere . . . His Blood Is Bibline"

Three times Bunyan says that the key was in Christians "*chest* pocket" or simply his "chest." I take this to mean that Christian had hidden it in his heart by memorization and that it was now accessible in prison for precisely this reason. This is how the promises sustained and strengthened Bunyan. He was filled with Scripture. Everything he wrote was saturated with Bible. He poured over his English Bible, which he had most of the time. This is why he can say of his writings, "I have not for these things fished in other men's waters; my Bible and Concordance are my only library in my writings."

Charles Spurgeon put it like this:

> *He had studied our Authorized Version . . . till his whole being was saturated with Scripture; and though his writings . . . continually make us feel and say, 'Why, this man is a living Bible!' Prick him anywhere; and you will find that his blood is Bibline, the very essence of the Bible flows*

> *from him. He cannot speak with out quoting a text, for his soul is full of the word of God.*

Bunyan reverenced the word of God and trembled at the prospect of dishonoring it. "Let me die . . . with the Philistines (Judg 16:30) rather than deal corruptly with the blessed word of God." This, in the end, is why Bunyan is still with us today rather than disappearing into the mist of history. He is with us and ministering to us because he reverenced the word of God and was so permeated by it that his blood is "Bibline" and that "the essence of the Bible flows from him."

And this is what he has to show us. That "to live upon God who is invisible" is to live upon God in his word. And to serve and suffer out of a life in God is to serve and suffer out of a life drenched with the word of God. This is how we shall live, this is how we shall suffer, and this is how we shall help those we love get safely to the Celestial City. We will woo them with the word. We will say to them what Bunyan said to his people:

> *God hath strewed all the way from the gate of hell, where thou wast, to the gate of heaven, whither thou art going, with flowers out of his own garden. Behold how the promises, invitations, calls, and encouragements, like lilies, lie round about thee! Take heed that thou dost not tread them under thy foot.*

PREFACE

John Newton, 1776

The writings of Mr. Bunyan need no recommendatory preface. The various editions they have passed through, and the different languages into which many of them have been translated, sufficiently prove that the gifts of God which were in him, have, by the divine blessing, been made very acceptable and useful to the churches. Though he was called to the knowledge and ministry of the gospel from a low state of life, as well as from a vicious course of conversation, and was unfurnished with human literature, the Lord, the great, the effectual, the only effectual teacher, made him, in an eminent degree, an able and successful minister of the New Testament. It is probable that only the people to whom he personally preached would have been benefited by his zeal and experience, had not the Lord permitted the rage of his enemies to prevail against him for a season. He lived in more trying days than those in which our lot is fallen. For preaching the word of life to sinners, he was sentenced to perpetual banishment, but what he actually suffered was imprisonment for more than twelve years. But his spirit was not bound. Though secluded from his public work, he could not be idle. He applied himself to writing books, and most of the treatises, by which being dead he still speaketh (in number about threescore) were composed during his confinement in Bedford Jail. Thus his adversaries themselves contributed to extend his usefulness by the very methods they took to prevent it. And (as in the apostle's case) the things that happened to him, proved rather to the furtherance than the hindrance of the gospel.

His books, though devoid of that art and those ornaments, on which writers who seek the praise of men lay so great a stress, have been, and still are highly esteemed by those who have a taste for divine truth; and greatly instrumental, in the hands of the Holy Spirit, to the awakening of the careless, and the encouragement of those who are seeking salvation. And we doubt not but they will be farther owned of God for these purposes, to many who are yet unborn. But as among the stars one excelleth another in glory, so of all our author's writings, there is no one perhaps so universally and deservedly admired as his *Pilgrim's Progress*, in which he gives a delineation of the Christian life under the idea of a journey or a pilgrimage, from the City of Destruction to the heavenly Jerusalem. In this treatise he appears not only as a writer well instructed in the mysteries of the kingdom, but a man of real genius. Though he had not a learned education, God had given him considerable natural abilities, a lively invention, a penetrating spirit, a strong judgment, and his style, though plain and simple, is remarkably clear, animated, and engaging. By the exercises through which the Lord led him, and a close study of the Word of God, he acquired a singular knowledge of the human heart, and its various workings, both in a state of nature and grace, and of the various snares and dangers to which a believer is exposed from the men and things of the world, and the subtlety of Satan. These fruits of his experience and observation he has exhibited in a very pleasing and instructive manner in his pilgrim, which may be considered as a map of the Christian profession in its present mixed state, while the wheat and the tares are growing in the same field. A map, so exactly drawn, that we can hardly meet with a case or character, amidst the vast variety of persons and incidents, that daily occur to our observation, to which we cannot easily point out a counterpart in the pilgrim. And he is peculiarly happy in fixing the attention of his readers: many have read this book with a kind of rapturous pleasure, though they have not understood the authors design, (which only they who have the eyes of their minds enlightened by the Spirit of God can fully enter into) and they who understand it best, and who have read it often, usually find fresh pleasure and instruction upon every perusal.

As many persons who have read this allegory, though they find benefit from the whole, are at a loss to determine the author's meaning in some particular parts of his representation, an edition containing some brief notes to illustrate the more difficult passages, has been long desired. An attempt of this kind is now submitted to the public. The annotator does not pretend to be positive that he has always precisely taken up the thought the author had upon his mind at the time of writing, though he thinks there are but few places in which he is in danger of greatly missing it. He hopes however that he has proposed no illustration but what will be found agreeable to the analogy of faith and the experience of believers.

The unusual demand for the *Pilgrim's Progress* upon its first appearance, induced the author some time after to send forth a second part. In which there are many beautiful passages that sufficiently demonstrate it to be the work of the same masterly hand. But the plan of that which is now called the First Part, was so comprehensive, and so well executed, that the subject was too much exhausted to admit of a Second Part, capable of standing in competition with the former. It is upon the whole greatly inferior to it, though a few pages here and there might be selected, which, for their beauty, propriety, and energy, almost deserve the epithet of inimitable (See the character of Mr. Fearing, and Standfast's discourse when in the river).

There is a small book in print which bears the title of the third part of the *Pilgrim's Progress*. It can hardly be necessary to inform any but those who have not read it, that this pretended third part, with Mr. Bunyan's name, is a gross imposition on the public, and that the title is almost the only part of it which bears any resemblance to Bunyan's Pilgrim, excepting when the writer has borrowed the same names. But Bunyan's spirit and manner he could not borrow, and his principles he openly contradicts. A common hedge-stake deserves as much to be compared to Aaron's rod, which yielded blossoms and almonds, as this poor performance to be obtruded upon the world under the title of the third part of the *Pilgrim's Progress*.

Thus much concerning our book: Let the v close with a word to the reader's heart. If you are not convinced of sin, and led by the Spirit to seek Jesus, notwithstanding the notes, the *Pilgrim* will still be a riddle to you. A well-wisher to your soul assures you, that whether you know these things or not, they are important realities. The *Pilgrim* is a parable, but it has an interpretation in which you are nearly concerned. If you are living in sin, you are in the City of Destruction. O hear the warning voice! "Flee from the wrath to come." Pray that the eyes of your mind may be opened, then you will see your danger, and gladly follow the shining light of the word, till you enter by Christ, the straight gate, into the way of salvation. If death surprise you before you get into this road, you are lost forever.

If you are indeed asking the way to Zion with your face thitherward, I bid you good speed. Behold an open door is set before you, which none can shut. Yet prepare to endure hardship, for the way lies through many tribulations. There are hills and valleys to be passed, lions and dragons to be met with, but the Lord of the hill will guide and guard his people. "Put on the whole armor of God, fight the good fight of faith." Beware of the Flatterer. Beware of the Enchanted Ground. See the Land of Beulah, yea, the city of Jerusalem itself is before you:

There Jesus the forerunner waits.

To welcome travelers home.

JOHN NEWTON.

THE PILGRIM'S PROGRESS

In The Similitude of a Dream

BY JOHN BUNYAN

"I have used similitudes."—Hosea 12:10

THE JAIL

As I walked through the wilderness of this world, I lighted on a certain place, where was a den; and I laid me down in that place to sleep: and as I slept, I dreamed a dream. I dreamed, and, behold, "I saw a man clothed with rags, standing in a certain place, with his face from his own house, a book in his hand, and a great burden upon his back."[1] I looked, and saw him open the book, and read therein; and as he read, he wept and trembled; and not being able longer to contain, he brake out with a lamentable cry, saying, "What shall I do?"[2]

In this plight, therefore, he went home, and refrained himself as long as he could, that his wife and children should not perceive his distress; but he could not be silent long, because that his trouble increased. Wherefore at length he brake his mind to his wife and children; and thus he began to talk to them: "O my dear wife," said he, "and you, the children of my bowels, I, your dear friend, am in myself undone, by reason of a burden that lieth hard upon me; moreover, I am for certain informed that this our city will be burned with fire from Heaven; in which fearful overthrow, both myself, with thee, my wife, and you, my sweet babes, shall miserably come to ruin, except (the which yet I see not) some way of escape can be found, whereby we may be

1 Isa. 64:6; Luke 14:33; Psa. 38:4; Hab. 2:2; Acts 16:31

2 Acts 2:37

delivered." At this, his relations were sore amazed; not for that they believed that what he had said to them was true, but because they thought that some frenzy distemper had got into his head; therefore, it drawing towards night, and they hoping that sleep might settle his brains, with all haste they got him to bed. But the night was as troublesome to him as the day; wherefore, instead of sleeping, he spent it in sighs and tears. So when the morning was come, they would know how he did; he told them, worse and worse; he also set to talking to them again, but they began to be hardened. They also thought to drive away his distemper by harsh and surly carriages to him. Sometimes they would deride, sometimes they would chide, and sometimes they would quite neglect him. Wherefore he began to retire himself to his chamber to pray for, and pity them, and also to condole his own misery. He would also walk solitarily in the fields, sometimes reading, and sometimes praying; and thus for some days he spent his time.

Now I saw upon a time, when he was walking in the fields, that he was, as he was wont, reading in his book, and greatly distressed in his mind; and as he read, he burst out, as he had done before, crying, "What shall I do to be saved?"[3]

I saw also that he looked this way and that way, as if he would run; yet he stood still, because, as I perceived, he could not tell which way to go. I looked then, and saw a man named Evangelist coming to him, who asked, "Where fore dost thou cry?"

He answered, Sir, I perceive, by the book in my hand, that I am condemned to die, and after that to come to judg-

3 Acts 16:30, 31

ment, and I find that I am not willing[4] to do the first, nor able[5] to do the second.

Then said Evangelist, Why not willing to die, since this life is attended with so many evils? The man answered, because I fear that this burden that is upon my back will sink me lower than the grave; and I shall fall into Tophet.[6] And, Sir, if I be not fit to go to prison, I am not fit, I am sure, to go to judgment, and from thence to execution; and the thoughts of these things make me cry.

4 Job 16:21, 22

5 Ezek. 22:14

6 Isa. 30:33

CONVICTION OF THE NECESSITY OF FLYING

Then said Evangelist, If this be thy condition, why standest thou still? He answered, Because I know not whither to go. Then he gave him a parchment roll, and there was written within, "Fly from the wrath to come".[7]

The man therefore, read it, and looking upon Evangelist very carefully, said, Whither must I fly? Then said Evangelist, pointing with his finger over a very wide field, Do you see yonder wicket gate?[8] The man said, No. Then said the other, Do you see yonder shining light?[9] He said, I think I do. Then said Evangelist, Keep that light in your eye, and go up directly thereto, so shalt thou see the gate; at which, when thou knockest, it shall be told thee what thou shalt do. So I saw in my dream that the man began to run. Now, he had not ran far from his own door, but his wife and children perceiving it, began to cry after him to return;[10] but the man put his fingers in his ears, and ran on, crying, Life! life! Eter-

7 Matt. 3:7

8 Matt. 7:13

9 Psa. 119:105; 2 Pet. 1:19

10 Luke 14:26

nal life! So he looked not behind him, but fled towards the middle of the plain.

The neighbours also came out to see him run, and as he ran, some mocked, others threatened, and some cried after him to return; and among those that did so, there were two that were resolved to fetch him back by force.[11] The name of the one was Obstinate, and the name of the other Pliable. Now by this time, the man was got a good distance from them; but, however, they were resolved to pursue him; which they did, and in a little time they overtook him. Then said the man, Neighbours, wherefore are ye come? They said, To persuade you to go back with us. But he said, That can by no means be. You dwell, said he, in the City of Destruction, the place also where I was born; I see it to be so; and dying there, sooner or later, you will sink lower than the grave, into a place that burns with fire and brimstone. Be content, good neighbours, and go along with me.

What, said Obstinate, and leave our friends and our comforts behind us?

Yes, said Christian, for that was his name, because that all "which you shall forsake"[12] is not worthy to be compared with a little of that which I am seeking to enjoy; and if you will go along with me, and hold it, you shall fare as I myself, for there, where I go, is enough and to spare.[13] Come away, and prove my words.

OBST. What are the things you seek, since you leave all the world to find them?

CHRISTIAN. I seek an "inheritance incorruptible, undefiled, and that fadeth not away"[14] and it is laid up in Heav-

11 Jer. 20:10
12 2 Cor. 4:18
13 Luke 15:17
14 1 Peter 1:4

en[15], and safe there, to be bestowed, at the time appointed, on them that diligently seek it. Read it so, if you will, in my book.

OBSTINATE. Tush, said Obstinate, away with your book; will you go back with us, or no?

CHRISTIAN. No, not I, saith the other; because I have laid my hand to the plough.[16]

OBSTINATE. Come, then, neighbour Pliable, let us turn again, and go home without him; there is a company of these crazed-headed coxcombs, that when they take a fancy by the end, are wiser in their own eyes than seven men that can render a reason.[17]

PLIABLE. Then said Pliable, Do not revile; if what the good Christian says is true, the things he looks after are better than ours; my heart inclines to go with my neighbour.

OBSTINATE. What! more fools still? Be ruled by me, and go back; who knows whither such a brain-sick fellow will lead you? Go back, go back, and be wise.

CHRISTIAN. Nay, but do thou come with thy neighbour Pliable: there are such things to be had which I spoke of, and many more glories besides; if you believe not me, read here in this book, and for the truth of what is expressed therein, behold, all is confirmed by the blood of Him that made it.[18]

PLIABLE. Well, neighbour Obstinate, saith Pliable, I begin to come to a point; I intend to go along with this good man, and to cast in my lot with him. But, my good companion, do you know the way to this desired place?

CHRISTIAN. I am directed by a man whose name is Evan-

15 Heb. 11:16

16 Luke 9:62

17 Prov. 26:16

18 Heb. 13:20, 21; 9:17–21

gelist, to speed me to a little gate that is before us, where we shall receive instructions about the way.

PLIABLE. Come then, good neighbour, let us be going. Then they went both together.

OBSTINATE. And I will go back to my place, said Obstinate; I will be no companion of such misled fantastical fellows.

THE SLOUGH OF DESPOND

Now I saw in my dream, that when Obstinate was gone back, Christian and Pliable went talking over the plain; and thus they began their discourse.

CHRISTIAN. Come, neighbour Pliable, how do you do? I am glad you are persuaded to go along with me; had even Obstinate himself but felt what I have felt, of the powers and terrors of what is yet unseen, he would not thus lightly have given us the back.

PLIABLE. Come, neighbour Christian, since there is none but us two here, tell me now further, what the things are, and how to be enjoyed, whither we are going

CHRISTIAN. I can better conceive of them with my mind, than speak of them with my tongue; but yet since you are desirous to know, I will read of them in my book.

PLIABLE. And do you think that the words of your book are certainly true?

CHRISTIAN. Yes, verily, for it was made by Him that cannot lie.[19]

PLIABLE. Well said. What things are they?

CHRISTIAN. There is an endless kingdom to be inhabit-

19 Titus 1:2

ed, and everlasting life to be given us, that we may inhabit that kingdom forever.[20]

PLIABLE. Well said. And what else?

CHRISTIAN. There are crowns of glory to be given us, and garments that will make us shine like the sun in the firmament of Heaven![21]

PLIABLE. This is very pleasant. And what else?

CHRISTIAN. There shall be no more crying, nor sorrow; for He that is owner of the place will wipe all tears from our eyes.[22]

PLIABLE. And what company shall we have there?

CHRISTIAN. There we shall be with seraphims, and Cherubims, creatures that will dazzle your eyes to look on them. There, also, you shall meet with thousands and ten thousands that have gone before us to that Place; none of them are hurtful, but loving and holy, everyone walking in the sight of God, and standing in His presence with acceptance forever; in a word, there we shall see the elders with their golden crowns; there we shall see the holy virgins with their golden harps; there we shall see men, that by the world were cut in pieces, burnt in flames, eaten of beasts, drowned in the seas, for the love that they bare to the Lord of the Place; all well, and clothed with immortality as with a garment.[23]

PLIABLE. The hearing of this is enough to ravish one's heart; but are these things to be enjoyed? How shall we get to be sharers thereof?

CHRISTIAN. The Lord, the Governor of the country, hath recorded, that in this book, the substance of which is,

20 Isa. 45:17; John 10:27–29

21 2 Tim. 4:8; Rev. 3:4; Matt. 13:43

22 Isa. 25:8; Rev. 7:17, 17; 21:4

23 Isa. 6:2; 1 Thess. 4:16, 17; Rev. 7:17; 4:4; 14:1–5; John 12:25; 2 Cor. 5:2–5

if we be truly willing to have it, He will bestow it upon us freely. [24]

PLIABLE. Well, my good companion, glad am I to hear of these things; come on, let us mend our pace.

CHRISTIAN. I cannot go so fast as I would, by reason of this burden that is on my back. Now I saw in my dream, that, just as they had ended this talk, they drew near to a very miry slough that was in the midst of the plain; and they, being heedless, did both fall suddenly into the bog. The name of the slough was Despond. Here, therefore, they wallowed for a time, being grievously bedaubed with the dirt; and Christian, because of the burden that was on his back, began to sink in the mire.

PLIABLE. Then said Pliable, Ah! neighbour Christian, where are you now?

CHRISTIAN. Truly, said Christian, I do not know.

PLIABLE. At that Pliable began to be offended, and angrily said to his fellow, Is this the happiness you have told me all this while of? If we have such ill speed at our first setting out, what may we expect betwixt this and our journey's end? May I get out again with my life, you shall possess the brave country alone for me. And with that he gave a desperate struggle or two, and got out of the mire on that side of the slough which was next to his own house: so away he went, and Christian saw him no more. Wherefore Christian was left to tumble in the Slough of Despond alone; but still he endeavoured to struggle to that side of the slough that was still further from his own house, and next to the wicket-gate; the which he did, but could not get out, because of the burden that was upon his back. But I beheld in my dream, that a man came to him, whose name was Help, and asked him what he did there?

24 Isa. 55:1, 2, 12; John 7:37; 6:37; Psa. 21:6; 22:17

CHRISTIAN. Sir, said Christian, I was bid go this way by a man called Evangelist, who directed me also to yonder gate, that I might escape the wrath to come. And as I was going thither, I fell in here.

HELP. But why did not you look for the steps?

CHRISTIAN. Fear followed me so hard, that I fled the next way, and fell in.

HELP. Then said he, Give me thy hand; so he gave him his hand, and he drew him out, and set him upon sound ground, and bid him go on his way.[25]

Then I stepped to him that plucked him out, and said, Sir, wherefore (since over this place is the way from the City of Destruction, to yonder gate) is it that this plat is not mended, that poor travelers might go thither with more security? And he said unto me, This miry slough is such a place as cannot be mended. It is the descent whither the scum and filth that attends conviction for sin, doth continually run, and therefore it is called the Slough of Despond: for still, as the sinner is awakened about his lost condition, there ariseth in his soul many fears, and doubts, and discouraging apprehensions, which all of them get together, and settle in this place. And this is the reason of the badness of this ground.

It is not the pleasure of the King that this place should remain so bad;[26] his labourers, also, have, by the directions of his Majesty's surveyors, been, for above these 1,600 years, employed about this patch of ground, if, perhaps, it might have been mended; yea, and to my knowledge, said he, here have been swallowed up at least 20,000 cart-loads; yea, millions of wholesome instructions, that have, at all seasons, been brought from all places of the King's dominions, and they that can tell, say, they are the best materials to make

25 Psa. 40:2

26 Isa. 35:3, 4

good ground of the place, if so be it might have been mended; but it is the Slough of Despond still; and so will be when they have done what they can.

True, there are, by the direction of the Lawgiver, certain good and substantial steps, placed even through the very midst of this slough; but at such time as this place doth much spew out its filth, as it doth against change of weather, these steps are hardly seen; or if they be, men, through the dizziness of their heads, step besides, and then they are bemired to purpose, notwithstanding the steps be there; but the ground is good, when they are once got in at the gate.[27]

Now I saw in my dream, that, by this time, Pliable was got home to his house again; so that his neighbours came to visit him; and some of them called him wise man for coming back, and some called him fool for hazarding himself with Christian; others, again, did mock at his cowardliness, saying, "Surely, since you began to venture, I would not have been so base to have given out for a few difficulties." So Pliable sat sneaking among them. But, at last, he got more confidence, and then they all turned their tales, and began to deride poor Christian behind his back. And thus much concerning Pliable.

Now as Christian was walking solitarily by himself, he espied one afar off come crossing over the field to meet him; and their hap was to meet just as they were crossing the way of each other. The gentleman's name that met him was Mr. Worldly-wiseman; he dwelt in the town of Carnal Policy, a very great town, and also hard by from whence Christian came. This man, then, meeting with Christian, and having some inkling of him, for Christian's setting forth from the City of Destruction was much noised abroad, not only in the town where he dwelt, but, also, it began to be the town-

27 1 Sam. 12:23

talk in some other places. Master Worldly-wiseman, therefore, having some guess of him, by beholding his laborious going, by observing his sighs and groans, and the like, began thus to enter into some talk with Christian.

WORLD. How now, good fellow, whither away after this burdened manner?

CHRISTIAN. A burdened manner, indeed, as ever, I think, poor creature had! And whereas you ask me, Whither away? I tell you, Sir, I am going to yonder wicket-gate before me; for there, as I am informed, I shall be put into a way to be rid of my heavy burden.

WORLD. Hast thou a wife and children?

CHRISTIAN. Yes; but I am so laden with this burden, that I cannot take that pleasure in them as formerly; methinks I am as if I had none.[28]

WORLD. Wilt thou hearken unto me if I give thee counsel?

CHRISTIAN. If it be good, I will; for I stand in need of good counsel.

WORLD. I would advise thee, then, that thou with all speed get thyself rid of thy burden: for thou wilt never be settled in thy mind till then; nor canst thou enjoy the benefits of the blessing which God hath bestowed upon thee till then.

CHRISTIAN. That is that which I seek for, even to be rid of this heavy burden; but get it off myself, I cannot; nor is there any man in our country that can take it off my shoulders; therefore am I going this way, as I told you, that I may be rid of my burden.

WORLD. Who bid you go this way to be rid of thy burden?

CHRISTIAN. A man that appeared to me to be a very

28 1 Cor. 7:29

great and honourable person; his name, as I remember, is Evangelist.

WORLD. I beshrew him for his counsel! there is not a more dangerous and trouble some way in the world than is that unto which he hath directed thee; and that thou shalt find, if thou wilt be ruled by his counsel. Thou hast met with something, as I perceive already; for I see the dirt of the Slough of Despond is upon thee; but that slough is the beginning of the sorrows that do attend those that go on in that way. Hear me, I am older than thou; thou art like to meet with, on the way which thou goest, wearisomeness, painfulness, hunger, perils, nakedness, sword, lions, dragons, darkness, and, in a word, death, and what not! These things are certainly true, having been confirmed by many testimonies. And why should a man so carelessly cast away himself, by giving heed to a stranger?

CHRISTIAN. Why, Sir, this burden upon my back is more terrible to me than are all these things which you have mentioned; nay, methinks I care not what I meet with in the way, if so be I can also meet with deliverance from my burden.

WORLD. How camest thou by the burden at first?

CHRISTIAN. By reading this book in my hand.

WORLD. I thought so; and it is happened unto thee as to other weak men, who, meddling with things too high for them, do suddenly fall into thy distractions; which distractions do not only unman men, as thine, I perceive, has done thee, but they run them upon desperate ventures, to obtain they know not what.

CHRISTIAN. I know what I would obtain; it is ease for my heavy burden.

WORLD. But why wilt thou seek for ease this way, seeing so many dangers attend it? especially since, hadst thou but patience to hear me, I could direct thee to the obtaining of what thou desirest, without the dangers that thou in this way wilt run thyself into; yea, and the remedy is at hand. Besides, I will add, that, instead of those dangers, thou shalt meet with much safety, friendship, and content.

CHRISTIAN. Pray, Sir, open this secret to me.

WORLD. Why, in yonder village—the village is named Morality—there dwells a gentleman whose name is Legality, a very judicious man, and a man of a very good name, that has skill to help men off with such burdens as thine are from their shoulders: yea, to my knowledge, he hath done a great deal of good this way; aye, and besides, he hath skill to cure those that are somewhat crazed in their wits with their burdens. To him, as I said, thou mayest go, and be helped presently. His house is not quite a mile from this place, and if he should not be at home himself, he hath a pretty young man to his son, whose name is Civility, that can do it (to speak on) as well as the old gentleman himself; there, I say, thou mayest be eased of thy burden; and if thou art not minded to go back to thy former habitation, as, indeed, I would not wish thee, thou mayest send for thy wife and children to thee to this village, where there are houses now stand empty, one of which thou mayest have at reasonable rates; provision is there also cheap and good; and that which will make thy life the more happy is, to be sure, there thou shalt live by honest neighbours, in credit and good fashion.

Now was Christian somewhat at a stand; but presently he concluded, if this be true, which this gentleman hath said, my wisest course is to take his advice; and with that he thus further spoke.

CHRISTIAN. Sir, which is my way to this honest man's house?

WORLD. Do you see yonder hill?

CHRISTIAN. Yes, very well.

WORLD. By that hill you must go, and the first house you come at is his.

So Christian turned out of his way, to go to Mr. Legality's house for help; but, behold, when he was got now hard by the hill, it seemed so high, and also that side of it that was next the wayside, did hang so much over, that Christian was afraid to venture further, lest the hill should fall on his head; wherefore there he stood still, and wotted not what to do. Also his burden now seemed heavier to him, than while he was in his way. There came also flashes of fire out of the hill, that made Christian afraid that he should be burned.[29] Here, therefore, he sweat and did quake for fear.[30] And now he began to be sorry that he had taken Mr. Worldly-wiseman's counsel.

29 Exod. 19:16, 18
30 Heb. 12:21

EVANGELIST FINDETH CHRISTIAN UNDER MOUNT SINAI, AND LOOKETH SEVERELY UPON HIM

And with that he saw Evangelist coming to meet him; at the sight also of whom he began to blush for shame. So Evangelist drew nearer and nearer; and coming up to him, he looked upon him with a severe and dreadful countenance, and thus began to reason with Christian.

EVANGELIST. What dost thou here, Christian? said he: at which words Christian knew not what to answer; wherefore at present he stood speechless before him. Then said Evangelist further, Art not thou the man that I found crying without the walls of the City of Destruction?

CHRISTIAN. Yes, dear Sir, I am the man.

EVANGELIST. Did not I direct thee the way to the little wicket-gate?

CHRISTIAN. Yes, dear Sir, said Christian.

EVANGELIST. How is it, then, that thou art so quickly turned aside? for thou art now out of the way.

CHRISTIAN. I met with a gentleman so soon as I had got over the Slough of Despond, who persuaded me that I might, in the village before me, find a man that could take off my burden.

EVANGELIST. What was he?

CHRISTIAN. He looked like a gentleman, and talked much to me, and got me at last to yield; so I came hither: but when I beheld this hill, and how it hangs over the way, I suddenly made a stand, lest it should fall on my head.

EVANGELIST. What said that gentleman to you?

CHRISTIAN. Why, he asked me whither I was going? And I told him.

EVANGELIST. And what said he then?

CHRISTIAN. He asked me if I had a family? And I told him. But, said I, I am so loaden with the burden that is on my back, that I cannot take pleasure in them as formerly.

EVANGELIST. And what said he then?

CHRISTIAN. He bid me with speed get rid of my burden; and I told him it was ease that I sought. And, said I, I am therefore going to yonder gate, to receive further direction how I may get to the place of deliverance. So he said that he would show me a better way, and short, not so attended with difficulties as the way, Sir, that you set me in; which way, said he, will direct you to a gentleman's house that hath skill to take off these burdens: so I believed him, and turned out of that way into this, if haply I might be soon eased of my burden. But when I came to this place, and beheld things as they are, I stopped for fear (as I said) of danger: but I now know not what to do.

EVANGELIST. Then, said Evangelist, stand still a little, that I may show thee the words of God. So he stood trembling. Then said Evangelist, "See that ye refuse not Him that speaketh. For if they escaped not who refused Him that spake on earth, much more shall not we escape, if we turn away from Him that speaketh from Heaven".[31] He said, moreover, "Now the just shall live by faith: but if any man draw back, My soul shall have no pleasure in him".[32] He also did thus apply them: Thou art the man that art running into this misery; thou hast begun to reject the counsel of the Most High, and to draw back thy foot from the way of peace, even almost to the hazarding of thy perdition!

Then Christian fell down at his foot as dead, crying, "Woe is me, for I am undone!" At the sight of which, Evangelist caught him by the right hand, saying, "All manner of sin and blasphemies shall be forgiven unto men"; "Be not faithless, but believing".[33] Then did Christian again a little revive, and stood up trembling, as at first, before Evangelist.

Then Evangelist proceeded, saying, Give more earnest heed to the things that I shall tell thee of. I will now show thee who it was that deluded thee, and who it was also to whom he sent thee.—The man that met thee is one Worldly-wiseman, and rightly is he so called; partly, because he savoureth only the doctrine of this world[34], (therefore he always goes to the town of Morality to church); and partly because he loveth that doctrine best, for it saveth him best from the cross.[35] And because he is of this carnal temper, therefore he seeketh to prevent my ways, though right. Now there are three things in this man's counsel, that thou must utterly abhor.

1. His turning thee out of the way. 2. His labouring to render the cross odious to thee. And, 3. His setting thy feet in that way that leadeth unto the administration of death.

31 Heb. 12:25

32 Heb. 10:38

33 John 20:27

34 1 John 4:5

35 Gal. 6:12

First, Thou must abhor his turning thee out of the way; yea, and thine own consenting thereto: because this is to reject the counsel of God for the sake of the counsel of a Worldly-wiseman. The Lord says, "Strive to enter in at the strait gate"[36] the gate to which I send thee; for "strait is the gate which leadeth unto life, and few there be that find it."[37] From this little wicket-gate, and from the way thereto, hath this wicked man turned thee, to the bringing of thee almost to destruction; hate, therefore, his turning thee out of the way, and abhor thyself for hearkening to him.

Secondly, Thou must abhor his labouring to render the cross odious unto thee; for thou art to prefer it "before the treasures in Egypt."[38] Besides, the King of glory hath told thee, that he that "will save his life shall lose it"[39] And, "He that comes after Him, and hate not his father, and mother, and wife, and children, and brethren, and sisters, yea, and his own life also, he cannot be My disciple"[40] I say, therefore, for man to labour to persuade thee, that that shall be thy death, without which, THE TRUTH hath said, thou canst not have eternal life; this doctrine thou must abhor.

Thirdly, Thou must hate his setting of thy feet in the way that leadeth to the ministration of death. And for this thou must consider to whom he sent thee, and also how unable that person was to deliver thee from thy burden.

He to whom thou wast sent for ease, being by name Legality, is the son of the bond woman which now is, and is in bondage with her children;[41] and is, in a mystery, this

36 Luke 13:24

37 Matt. 7:14

38 Heb. 11:25, 26

39 Mark 8:35; John 12:25; Matt. 10:39

40 Luke 14:26

41 Gal. 4:21–27

mount Sinai, which thou hast feared will fall on thy head. Now, if she, with her children, are in bondage, how canst thou expect by them to be made free? This Legality, therefore, is not able to set thee free from thy burden. No man was as yet ever rid of his burden by him; no, nor ever is like to be: ye cannot be justified by the works of the law; for by the deeds of the law no man living can be rid of his burden: therefore, Mr. Worldly-wiseman is an alien, and Mr. Legality is a cheat; and for his son Civility, notwithstanding his simpering looks, he is but a hypocrite, and cannot help thee. Believe me, there is nothing in all this noise, that thou hast heard of these sottish men, but a design to beguile thee of thy salvation, by turning thee from the way in which I had set thee. After this, Evangelist called aloud to the heavens for confirmation of what he had said: and with that there came words and fire out of the mountain under which poor Christian stood, that made the hair of his flesh stand up. The words were thus pronounced: "As many as are of the works of the law are under the curse; for it is written, Cursed is everyone that continueth not in all things which are written in the book of the law to do them.[42]

Now Christian looked for nothing but death, and began to cry out lamentably; even cursing the time in which he met with Mr. Worldly-wiseman; still calling himself a thousand fools for hearkening to his counsel: he also was greatly ashamed to think that this gentleman's arguments, flowing only from the flesh, should have the prevalency with him as to cause him to forsake the right way. This done, he applied himself again to Evangelist, in words and sense as follows:—

CHRISTIAN. Sir, what think you? Is there hope? May I now go back, and go up to the wicket-gate? Shall I not be abandoned for this, and sent back from thence ashamed? I

42 Gal. 3:10

am sorry I have hearkened to this man's counsel. But may my sin be forgiven?

EVANGELIST. Then said Evangelist to him, Thy sin is very great, for by it thou hast committed two evils; thou hast forsaken the way that is good, to tread in forbidden paths; yet will the man at the gate receive thee, for he has good-will for men; only, said he, take heed that thou turn not aside again, "lest thou perish from the way, when His wrath is kindled but a little".[43] Then did Christian address himself to go back; and Evangelist, after he had kissed him, gave him one smile, and bid him God-speed. So he went on with haste, neither spake he to any man by the way; nor, if any asked him, would he vouchsafe them an answer. He went like one that was all the while treading on forbidden ground, and could by no means think himself safe, till again he was got into the way which he left, to follow Mr. Worldly-wiseman's counsel. So, in process of time, Christian got up to the gate. Now, over the gate there was written, "Knock, and it shall be opened unto you"[44]

He knocked, therefore, more than once or twice, saying—

"May I now enter here? Will He within
Open to sorry me, though I have been
An undeserving rebel? Then shall I
Not fail to sing His lasting praise on high."

At last there came a grave person to the gate, named Goodwill, who asked who was there? and whence he came? and what he would have?

CHRISTIAN. Here is a poor burdened sinner. I come

43 Psa. 2:12

44 Matt. 7:8

from the City of Destruction, but am going to Mount Zion, that I may be delivered from the wrath to come. I would, therefore, Sir, since I am informed that by this gate is the way thither, know if you are willing to let me in!

GOOD-WILL. I am willing with all my heart, said he; and with that he opened the gate.

So when Christian was stepping in, the other gave him a pull. Then said Christian, What means that? The other told him. A little distance from this gate, there is erected a strong castle, of which Beelzebub is the captain; from thence, both he and them that are with him shoot arrows at those that come up to this gate, if haply they may die before they can enter in.

Then said Christian, I rejoice and tremble. So when he was got in, the man of the gate asked him who directed him thither?

CHRISTIAN. Evangelist bid me come hither, and knock (as I did); and he said that you, Sir, would tell me what I must do.

GOOD-WILL. An open door is set before thee, and no man can shut it.

CHRISTIAN. Now I begin to reap the benefits of my hazards.

GOOD-WILL. But how is it that you came alone?

CHRISTIAN. Because none of my neighbours saw their danger, as I saw mine.

GOOD-WILL. Did any of them know of your coming?

CHRISTIAN. Yes; my wife and children saw me at the first, and called after me to turn again; also, some of my neighbours stood crying and calling after me to return; but I put my fingers in my ears, and so came on my way.

GOOD-WILL. But did none of them follow you, to persuade you to go back?

CHRISTIAN. Yes, both Obstinate and Pliable; but when

they saw that they could not prevail, Obstinate went railing back, but Pliable came with me a little way.

GOOD-WILL. But why did he not come through?

CHRISTIAN. We, indeed, came both together, until we came at the Slough of Despond, into the which we also suddenly fell. And then was my neighbour, Pliable, discouraged, and would not adventure further. Wherefore getting out again on that side next to his own house, he told me I should possess the brave country alone for him; so he went his way, and I came mine—he after Obstinate, and I to this gate.

GOOD-WILL. Then said Good-will, Alas, poor man! is the celestial glory of so small esteem with him, that he counteth it not worth running the hazards of a few difficulties to obtain it?

CHRISTIAN. Truly, said Christian, I have said the truth of Pliable, and if I should also say all the truth of myself, it will appear there is no betterment betwixt him and myself. It is true, he went back to his own house, but I also turned aside to go in the way of death, being persuaded thereto by the carnal arguments of one Mr. Worldly-wiseman.

GOOD-WILL. Oh! did he light upon you? What! he would have had you a sought for ease at the hands of Mr. Legality. They are, both of them, a very cheat. But did you take his counsel?

CHRISTIAN. Yes, as far as I durst; I went to find out Mr. Legality, until I thought that the mountain that stands by his house would have fallen upon my head; wherefore, there I was forced to stop.

GOOD-WILL. That mountain has been the death of many, and will be the death of many more; it is well you escaped being by it dashed in pieces.

CHRISTIAN. Why, truly, I do not know what had become of me there, had not Evangelist happily met me again, as I was musing in the midst of my dumps; but it was God's mercy that he came to me again, for else I had never come hither. But now I am come, such a one as I am, more fit, indeed, for death, by that mountain, than thus to stand talking with my Lord; but, O! what a favour is this to me, that yet I am admitted entrance here!

GOOD-WILL. We make no objections against any, notwithstanding all that they have done before they come hither. They are "in no wise cast out"[45] and therefore, good Christian, come a little way with me, and I will teach thee about the way thou must go. Look before thee; dost thou see this narrow way? THAT is the way thou must go; it was cast up by the patriarchs, prophets, Christ, and His Apostles; and it is as straight as a rule can make it. This is the way thou must go.

CHRISTIAN. But, said Christian, are there no turnings nor windings, by which a stranger may lose his way?

GOOD-WILL. Yes, there are many ways butt down upon this, and they are crooked and wide. But thus thou mayest distinguish the right from the wrong, the right only being straight and narrow.[46]

Then I saw in my dream, that Christian asked him further if he could not help him off with his burden that was upon his back; for as yet he had not got rid thereof, nor could he by any means get it off without help.

He told him, as to thy burden, be content to bear it, until thou comest to the place of deliverance; for there it will fall from thy back of itself.

Then Christian began to gird up his loins, and to address himself to his journey. So the other told him, That by that he was gone some distance from the gate, he would come at

45 John 6:37

46 Matt. 7:14

the house of the Interpreter; at whose door he should knock, and he would show him excellent things. Then Christian took his leave of his friend, and he again bid him God-speed.

Then he went on till he came at the house of the Interpreter, where he knocked over and over; at last one came to the door, and asked who was there.

CHRISTIAN. Sir, here is a traveler, who was bid by an acquaintance of the good man of this house to call here for my profit; I would therefore speak with the master of the house. So he called for the master of the house, who, after a little time, came to Christian, and asked him what he would have.

CHRISTIAN. Sir, said Christian, I am a man that am come from the City of Destruction, and am going to the Mount Zion; and I was told by the man that stands at the gate, at the head of this way, that if I called here, you would show me excellent things, such as would be a help to me in my journey.

INTERPRETER. Then said the Interpreter, Come in; I will show thee that which will be profitable to thee. So He commanded His man to light the candle, and bid Christian follow Him: so He had him into a private room, and bid His man open a door; the which when he had done, Christian saw the picture of a very grave person hang up against the wall; and this was the fashion of it. It had eyes lifted up to Heaven, the best of books in his hand, the law of truth was written upon his lips, the world was behind his back. It stood as if it pleaded with men, and a crown of gold did hang over its head.

CHRISTIAN. Then said Christian, What meaneth this?

INTERPRETER. The man whose picture this is, is one of a thousand; he can beget children,[47] travail in birth with chil-

47 1 Cor. 4:15

dren,[48] and nurse them himself when they are born. And whereas thou seest him with his eves lift up to Heaven, the best of books in his hand, and the law of truth writ on his lips, it is to show thee, that his work is to know and unfold dark things to sinners; even as also thou seest him stand as if he pleaded with men; and whereas thou seest the world as cast behind him, and that a crown hangs over his head, that is to show thee that slighting and despising the things that are present, for the love that he hath to his Master's service, he is sure in the world that comes next to have glory for his reward. Now, said the Interpreter, I have showed thee this picture first, because the man whose picture this is, is the only man whom the Lord of the place whither thou art going, hath authorized to be thy guide in all difficult places thou mayest meet with in the way; wherefore, take good heed to what I have showed thee, and bear well in thy mind what thou hast seen, lest in thy journey thou meet with some that pretend to lead thee right, but their way goes down to death.

Then He took him by the hand, and led him into a very large parlour that was full of dust, because never swept; the which, after He had reviewed a little while, the Interpreter called for a man to sweep. Now, when he began to sweep, the dust began so abundantly to fly about, that Christian had almost therewith been choked. Then said the Interpreter to a damsel that stood by, Bring hither the water, and sprinkle the room; the which, when she had done, it was swept and cleansed with pleasure.

CHRISTIAN. Then said Christian, What means this?

INTERPRETER. The Interpreter answered, This parlour is the heart of a man that was never sanctified by the sweet grace of the Gospel; the dust is his original sin and inward

48 Gal. 4:19

corruptions, that have defiled the whole man. He that began to sweep at first, is the Law; but she that brought water, and did sprinkle it, is the Gospel. Now, whereas thou sawest, that so soon as the first began to sweep, the dust did so fly about that the room by him could not be cleansed, but that thou wast almost choked therewith; this is to show thee, that the law, instead of cleansing the heart (by its working) from sin, doth revive, put strength into, and increase it in the soul, even as it doth discover and forbid it, for it doth not give power to subdue.[49]

Again, as thou sawest the damsel sprinkle the room with water, upon which it was cleansed with pleasure; this is to show thee, that when the Gospel comes in the sweet and precious influences thereof to the heart, then, I say, even as thou sawest the damsel lay the dust by sprinkling the floor with water, so is sin vanquished and subdued, and the soul made clean, through the faith of it, and consequently fit for the King of glory to inhabit.[50]

I saw, moreover, in my dream, that the Interpreter took him by the hand, and had him into a little room, where sat two little children, each one in his chair. The name of the elder was Passion, and the name of the other Patience. Passion seemed to be much discontented; but Patience was very quiet. Then Christian asked, What is the reason of the discontent of Passion? The Interpreter answered, The Governor of them would have him stay for his best things till the beginning of the next year; but he will have all now; but patience is willing to wait.

Then I saw that one came to Passion, and brought him a bag of treasure, and poured it down at his feet, the which he took up and rejoiced therein, and withal laughed Patience to

49 Rom. 7:6; 1 Cor. 15:56; Rom. 5:20

50 John 15:3; Eph. 5:26; Acts 15:9; Rom. 16:25, 26; John 15:13

scorn. But I beheld but a while, and he had lavished all away, and had nothing left him but rags.

CHRISTIAN. Then said Christian to the Interpreter, Expound this matter more fully to me.

INTERPRETER. So He said, These two lads are figures: Passion, of the men of this world; and Patience, of the men of that which is to come; for, as here thou seest, Passion will have all now this year, that is to say, in this world; so are the men of this world: they must have all their good things now, they cannot stay till next year, that is, until the next world, for their portion of good. That proverb, "A bird in the hand is worth two in the bush," is of more authority with them than are all the Divine testimonies of the good of the world to come. But as thou sawest that he had quickly lavished all away, and had presently left him nothing but rags; so will it be with all such men at the end of this world.

CHRISTIAN. Then said Christian, Now I see that Patience has the best wisdom, and that upon many accounts. First, Because he stays for the best things. Second, And also because he will have the glory of his, when the other has nothing but rags.

INTERPRETER. Nay, you may add another, to wit, the glory of the next world will never wear out; but these are suddenly gone. Therefore Passion had not so much reason to laugh at Patience, because he had his good things first, as Patience will have to laugh at Passion, because he had his best things last; for first must give place to last, because last must have his time to come; but last gives place to nothing; for there is not another to succeed. He, therefore, that hath his portion first, must needs have a time to spend it; but he that hath his portion last, must have it lastingly; therefore it is said of Dives, "Thou in thy lifetime receivedst thy good things, and likewise Lazarus evil things; but now he is comforted, and thou art tormented".[51]

CHRISTIAN. Then I perceive it is not best to covet things that are now, but to wait for things to come.

INTERPRETER. You say the truth: "For the things which are seen are temporal; but the things which are not seen are eternal".[52] But though this be so, yet since things present, and our fleshly appetite, are such near neighbours one to another; and again, because things to come, and carnal sense, are such strangers one to another; therefore it is that the first of these so suddenly fall into amity, and that distance is so continued between the second. Then I saw in my dream that the Interpreter took Christian by the hand, and led him into a place where was a fire burning against a wall, and one standing by it, always casting much water upon it, to quench it; yet did the fire burn higher and hotter.

Then said Christian, What means this?

The Interpreter answered, This fire is the work of grace that is wrought in the heart; he that casts water upon it, to extinguish and put it out, is the Devil; but in that thou seest the fire notwithstanding burn higher and hotter, thou shalt also see the reason of that. So he had him about to the backside of the wall, where be saw a man with a vessel of oil in his hand, of the which He did also continually cast, but secretly, into the fire.

Then said Christian, What means this?

The Interpreter answered, This is Christ, who continually, with the oil of his grace, maintains the work already begun in the heart: by the means of which, notwithstanding what the devil can do, the souls of His people prove gracious

51 Luke 16:25

52 2 Cor. 4:18

still.[53] And in that thou sawest that the man stood behind the wall to maintain the fire, that is to teach thee that it is hard for the tempted to see how this work of grace is maintained in the soul.

I saw also, that the Interpreter took him again by the hand, and led him into a pleasant place, where was builded a stately palace, beautiful to behold; at the sight of which Christian was greatly delighted; he saw also, upon the top thereof, certain persons walking, who were clothed all in gold.

Then said Christian, May we go in thither?

Then the Interpreter took him, and led him up towards the door of the palace; and behold, at the door stood a great company of men, as desirous to go in, but durst not. There also sat a man at a little distance from the door, at a table-side, with a book and his inkhorn before him, to take the name of him that should enter therein; he saw also, that in the doorway stood many men in armour to keep it, being resolved to do the men that would enter what hurt and mischief they could. Now was Christian somewhat in amaze. At last, when every man started back for fear of the armed men, Christian saw a man of a very stout countenance come up to the man that sat there to write, saying, "Set down my name, Sir": the which when he had done, he saw the man draw his sword, and put an helmet upon his head, and rush toward the door upon the armed men, who laid upon him with deadly force: but the man, not at all discouraged, fell to cutting and hacking most fiercely. So after he had received and given many wounds to those that attempted to keep him out, he cut his way through them all,[54] and pressed forward into the palace, at which there was a pleasant voice

53 2 Cor. 12:9

54 Acts 14:22

heard from those that were within, even of those that walked upon the top of the palace, saying—

> *"Come in, come in;*
> *Eternal glory thou shalt win."*

So he went in, and was clothed with such garments as they. Then Christian smiled and said, I think verily I know the meaning of this.

Now, said Christian, let me go hence. Nay, stay, said the Interpreter, till I have showed thee a little more, and after that thou shalt go on thy way. So He took him by the hand again, and led him into a very dark room, where there sat a man in an iron cage.

Now the man, to look on, seemed very sad; he sat with his eyes looking down to the ground, his hands folded together, and he sighed as if he would break his heart. Then said Christian, What means this? At which the Interpreter bid him talk with the man.

Then Said Christian to the man, What art thou? The man answered, I am what I was not once.

CHRISTIAN. What wast thou once?

MAN. The man said, I was once a fair and flourishing professor, both in mine own eyes, and also in the eyes of others; I once was, as I thought, fair for the Celestial City, and had then even joy at the thoughts that I should get thither.[55]

CHRISTIAN. Well, but what art thou now?

MAN. I am now a man of despair, and am shut up in it, as in this iron cage. I cannot get out. O now I cannot!

CHRISTIAN. But how camest thou in this condition?

MAN. I left off to watch and be sober; I laid the reins upon the neck of my lusts; I sinned against the light of the

55 Luke 8:13

Word, and the goodness of God; I have grieved the Spirit, and He is gone; I tempted the devil, and he is come to me; I have provoked God to anger, and He has left me; I have so hardened my heart, that I cannot repent.

Then said Christian to the Interpreter, But is there no hope for such a man as this? Ask him, said the Interpreter. Nay, said Christian, pray Sir, do you.

INTERPRETER. Then said the Interpreter, Is there no hope, but you must be kept in the iron cage of despair?

MAN. No, none at all.

INTERPRETER. Why, the Son of the Blessed is very pitiful.

MAN. I have crucified Him to myself afresh;[56] I have despised His person;[57] I have despised His righteousness; I have "counted His blood an unholy thing"; I have "done despite to the Spirit of grace".[58] Therefore I have shut myself out of all the promises, and there now remains to me nothing but threatenings, dreadful threatenings, fearful threatenings of certain judgment and fiery indignation, which shall devour me as an adversary.

INTERPRETER. For what did you bring yourself into this condition?

MAN. For the lusts, pleasures, and profits of this world; in the enjoyment of which I did then promise myself much delight; but now every one of those things also bite me, and gnaw me like a burning worm.

INTERPRETER. But canst thou not now repent and turn?

MAN. God hath denied me repentance. His Word gives me no encouragement to believe; yea, Himself hath shut me up in this iron cage; nor can all the men in the world let me

56 Heb. 4:6

57 Luke 19:14

58 Heb. 10:28, 29

out. O eternity! eternity! how shall I grapple with the misery that I must meet with in eternity!

INTERPRETER. Then said the Interpreter to Christian, Let this man's misery be remembered by thee, and be an everlasting caution to thee.

CHRISTIAN. Well, said Christian, this is fearful! God help me to watch and be sober, and to pray that I may shun the cause of this man's misery! Sir, is it not time for me to go on my way now?

INTERPRETER. Tarry till I shall show thee one thing more, and then thou shalt go on thy way.

So He took Christian by the hand again, and led him into a chamber, where there was one rising out of bed; and as he put on his raiment, he shook and trembled. Then said Christian, Why doth this man thus tremble? The Interpreter then bid him tell to Christian the reason of his so doing. So he began and said, This night, as I was in my sleep, I dreamed, and behold the heavens grew exceeding black; also it thundered and lightened in most fearful wise, that it put me into an agony; so I looked up in my dream, and saw the clouds rack at an unusual rate, upon which I heard a great sound of a trumpet, and saw also a man sit upon a cloud, attended with the thousands of Heaven; they were all in flaming fire: also the heavens were in a burning flame. I heard then a voice saying, "Arise, ye dead, and come to judgment"; and with that the rocks rent, the graves opened, and the dead that were therein came forth. Some of them were exceeding glad, and looked upward; and some sought to hide themselves under the mountains.[59] Then I saw the man that sat upon the cloud open the book, and bid the world draw near. Yet there was, by reason of a fierce flame

59 1 Cor. 15:52; 1 Thess. 4:16; Jude 14; John 5:28, 29; 2 Thess. 1:7, 8; Rev. 20:11–14; Isa. 26:21; Micah 7:16, 17; Psa. 95:1–3; Dan. 7:10

which issued out and came from before him, a convenient distance betwixt him and them, as betwixt the judge and the prisoners at the bar.[60] I heard it also proclaimed to them that attended on the man that sat on the cloud, "Gather together the tares, the chaff, and stubble, and cast them into the burning lake"[61] And with that, the bottomless pit opened, just whereabouts I stood; out of the mouth of which there came, in an abundant manner, smoke and coals of fire, with hideous noises. It was also said to the same persons, "Gather My wheat into the garner".[62] And with that I saw many catched up and carried away into the clouds, but I was left behind.[63] I also sought to hide myself, but I could not, for the man that sat upon the cloud still kept his eye upon me: my sins also came into my mind; and my conscience did accuse me on every side.[64] Upon this I awaked from my sleep.

CHRISTIAN. But what was it that made you so afraid of this sight?

MAN. Why, I thought that the day of judgment was come, and that I was not ready for it: but this frighted me most, that the angels gathered up several, and left me behind; also the pit of hell opened her mouth just where I stood. My conscience, too, afflicted me; and, as I thought, the Judge had always his eye upon me, showing indignation in his countenance.

Then said the Interpreter to Christian, Hast thou considered all these things?

CHRISTIAN. Yes, and they put me in hope and fear.

INTERPRETER. Well, keep all things so in thy mind that

60 Mal. 3:2, 3; Dan. 7:9, 10

61 Matt. 3:12; 13:30; Mal. 4:1

62 Luke 3:17

63 1 Thess. 4:16, 17

64 Rom. 2:14, 15

they may be as a goad in thy sides, to prick thee forward in the way thou must go. Then Christian began to gird up his loins, and to address himself to his journey. Then said the Interpreter, The Comforter be always with thee, good Christian, to guide thee in the way that leads to the City. So Christian went on his way, saying—

"Here I have seen things rare and profitable;
Things pleasant, dreadful, things to make me stable
In what I have begun to take in hand;
Then let me think on them, and understand
Wherefore they showed me were, and let me be
Thankful, O good Interpreter, to thee."

PROCEEDS TO THE CROSS

Now I saw in my dream, that the highway up which Christian was to go, was fenced on either side with a wall, and that wall was called Salvation.[65] Up this way, therefore, did burdened Christian run, but not without great difficulty, because of the load on his back.

He ran thus till he came to a place somewhat ascending, and upon that place stood a cross, and a little below, in the bottom, a sepulchre. So I saw in my dream, that just as Christian came up with the cross, his burden loosed from off his shoulders, and fell from off his back, and began to tumble, and so continued to do, till it came to the mouth of the sepulchre, where it fell in, and I saw it no more.

Then was Christian glad and lightsome, and said, with a merry heart, "He hath given me rest by His sorrow, and life by His death." Then he stood still awhile to look and wonder; for it was very surprising to him, that the sight of the cross should thus ease him of his burden. He looked, therefore, and looked again, even till the springs that were in his head sent the waters down his checks.[66] Now, as he stood looking and weeping, behold three Shining Ones came to him and saluted him with "Peace be to thee." So the first

65 Isa. 26:1

66 Zech. 12:10

said to him, "Thy sins be forgiven thee:[67] the second stripped him of his rags, and clothed him "with change of raiment";[68] the third also set a mark in his forehead, and gave him a roll with a seal upon it, which he bade him look on as he ran, and that he should give it in at the Celestial Gate (Eph. 1:13). So they went their way. Then Christian gave three leaps for joy, and went on singing—

Thus far I did come laden with my sin;
Nor could aught ease the grief that I was in
Till I came hither: What a place is this!
Must here be the beginning of my bliss?
Must here the burden fall from off my back
Must here the strings that bound it to me crack?
Blest cross! blest sepulchre! blest rather be
The man that there was put to shame for me!

I saw then in my dream, that he went on thus, even until he came at a bottom, where he saw, a little out of the way, three men fast asleep, with fetters upon their heels. The name of the one was Simple, another Sloth, and the third Presumption.

67 Mark 2:15
68 Zech. 3:4

CHRISTIAN SALUTED BY THE THREE SHINING ONES

Christian then seeing them lie in this case, went to them, if peradventure he might awake them, and cried, You are like them that sleep on the top of a mast, for the Dead Sea is under you—a gulf that hath no bottom.[69] Awake, therefore, and come away; be willing also, and I will help you off with your irons. He also told them, If he that "goeth about like a roaring lion" comes by, you will certainly become a prey to his.[70] With that they looked upon him, and began to reply in this sort: Simple said, "I see no danger"; Sloth said, "Yet a little more sleep"; and Presumption said, "Every fat must stand upon its own bottom; what is the answer else that I should give thee?" And so they lay down to sleep again, and Christian went on his way.

Yet was he troubled to think that men in that danger should so little esteem the kindness of him that so freely offered to help them, both by awakening of them, counseling of them, and proffering to help them off with their irons. And as he was troubled thereabout, he espied two men come tumbling over the wall, on the left hand of the narrow way;

69 Prov. 23:34

70 1 Peter 5:8

and they made up apace to him. The name of the one was Formalist, and the name of the other Hypocrisy. So, as I said, they drew up unto him, who thus entered with them into discourse.

CHRISTIAN. Gentlemen, whence came you, and whither go you?

FORMALIST and HYPOCRISY. We were born in the land of Vain-glory, and are going for praise to Mount Sion.

CHRISTIAN. Why came you not in at the gate, which standeth at the beginning of the way? Know you not that it is written, that he that cometh not in by the door, "but climbeth up some other way, the same is a thief and a robber?".[71]

FORMALIST and HYPOCRISY. They said, that to go to the gate for entrance was, by all their countrymen, counted too far about; and that, therefore, their usual way was to make a short cut of it, and to climb over the wall, as they had done.

CHRISTIAN. But will it not be counted a trespass against the Lord of the city whither we are bound, thus to violate His revealed will?

FORMALIST and HYPOCRISY. They told him, that, as for that, he needed not to trouble his head thereabout; for what they did, they had custom for; and could produce, if need were, testimony that would witness it for more than a thousand years.

CHRISTIAN. But, said Christian, will your practice stand a trial at law?

FORMALIST and HYPOCRISY. They told him, That custom, it being of so long a standing as above a thousand years, would, doubtless, now be admitted as a thing legal by any impartial judge; and beside, said they, if we get into the way, what's matter which way we get in? if we are in, we are in;

71 John 10:1

thou art but in the way, who, as we perceive, came in at the gate; and we, are also in the way, that came tumbling over the wall; wherein, now, is thy condition better than ours?

CHRISTIAN. I walk by the rule of my Master; you walk by the rude working of your fancies. You are counted thieves already, by the Lord of the way; therefore, I doubt you will not be found true men at the end of the way. You come in by yourselves, without His direction; and shall go out by yourselves, without His mercy.

To this they made him but little answer; only they bid him look to himself. Then I saw that they went on every man in his way, without much conference one with another; save that these two men told Christian, that as to laws and ordinances, they doubted not but they should as conscientiously do them as he; therefore, said they, we see not wherein thou differest from us, but by the coat that is on thy back, which was, as we trow given thee by some of thy neighbours, to hide the shame of thy nakedness.

CHRISTIAN. By laws and ordinances you will not be saved, since you came not in by the door.[72] And as for this coat that is on my back, it was given me by the Lord of the place whither I go; and that, as you say, to cover my nakedness with. And I take it as a token of His kindness to me; for I had nothing but rags before. And, besides, thus I comfort myself as I go: Surely, think I, when I come to the gate of the city, the Lord thereof will know me for good, since I have His coat on my back—a coat that He gave me in the day that He stripped me of my rags. I have, moreover, a mark in my forehead, of which, perhaps, you have taken no notice, which one of my Lord's most intimate associates fixed there in the day that my burden fell off my shoulders. I will tell you, moreover, that I had then given me a roll, sealed, to

72 Gal. 1:16

comfort me by reading, as I go on the way; I was also bid to give it in at the Celestial Gate, in token of my certain going in after it; all which things, I doubt, you want, and want them because you came not in at the gate.

To these things they gave him no answer; only they looked upon each other, and laughed. Then I saw that they went on all, save that Christian kept before, who had no more talk but with himself, and that sometimes sighingly and sometimes comfortably also he would be often reading in the roll that one of the Shining Ones gave him, by which he was refreshed.

THE HILL OF DIFFICULTY

I beheld, then, that they all went on till they came to the foot of the Hill Difficulty; at the bottom of which was a spring. There were also in the same place two other ways besides that which came straight from the gate; one turned to the left hand, and the other to the right, at the bottom of the hill; but the narrow way lay right up the hill, and the name of the going up the side of the hill is called Difficulty. Christian now went to the spring, and drank thereof, to refresh himself,[73] and then began to go up the hill, saying—

"The hill, though high, I covet to ascend,
The difficulty will not me offend;
For I perceive the way to life lies here.
Come, pluck up heart, let's neither faint nor fear;
Better, though difficult, the right way to go,
Than wrong, though easy, where the end is Woe."

The other two also came to the foot of the hill; but when they saw that the hill was steep and high, and that there were two other ways to go; and supposing also that these two ways might meet again, with that up which Christian went, on the other side of the hill; therefore they were resolved to

73 Isa. 49:10

go in those ways. Now the name of one of those ways was Danger, and the name of the other Destruction. So the one took the way which is called Danger, which led him into a great wood, and the other took directly up the way to Destruction, which led him into a wide field, full of dark mountains, where he stumbled and fell, and rose no more.

I looked, then, after Christian, to see him go up the hill, where I perceived he fell from running to going, and from going to clambering upon his hands and his knees, because of the steepness of the place. Now, about the midway to the top of the hill was a pleasant arbour, made by the Lord of the hill for the refreshing of weary travelers; thither, therefore, Christian got, where also he sat down to rest him. Then he pulled his roll out of his bosom, and read therein to his comfort; he also now began afresh to take a review of the coat or garment that was given him as he stood by the cross. Thus pleasing himself awhile, he at last fell into a slumber, and thence into a fast sleep, which detained him in that place until it was almost night; and in his sleep his roll fell out of his hand. Now, as he was sleeping, there came one to him, and awaked him, saying, "Go to the ant, thou sluggard; consider her ways, and be wise".[74] And with that Christian suddenly started up, and sped him on his way, and went apace, till be came to the top of the hill.

Now, when he was got up to the top of the hill, there came two men running to meet him amain; the name of the one was Timorous, and of the other Mistrust; to whom Christian said, Sirs, what's the matter? You run the wrong way. Timorous answered, that they were going to the City of Zion, and had got up that difficult place; but, said he, the further we go, the more danger we meet with; wherefore we turned, and are going back again.

74 Prov. 6:6

Yes, said Mistrust, for just before us lie a couple of lions in the way, whether sleeping or waking we know not, and we could not think, if we came within reach, but they would presently pull us in pieces.

CHRISTIAN. Then said Christian, You make me afraid, but whither shall I fly to be safe? If I go back to mine own country, that is prepared for fire and brimstone, and I shall certainly perish there. If I can get to the Celestial City, I am sure to be in safety there. I must venture. To go back is nothing but death; to go forward is fear of death, and life everlasting beyond it. I will yet go forward. So Mistrust and Timorous ran down the hill, and Christian went on his way. But, thinking again of what he heard from the men, be felt in his bosom for his roll, that he might read therein, and be comforted; but he felt, and found it not. Then was Christian in great distress, and knew not what to do; for he wanted that which used to relieve him, and that which should have been his pass into the Celestial City. Here, therefore, he began to be much perplexed, and knew not what to do. At last, he bethought himself, that he had slept in the arbour that is on the side of the hill; and, falling down upon his knees, he asked God's forgiveness for that his foolish act, and then went back to look for his roll. But all the way he went back, who can sufficiently set forth the sorrow of Christian's heart! Sometimes he sighed, sometimes he wept, and oftentimes he chid himself for being so foolish to fall asleep in that place, which was erected only for a little refreshment for his weariness. Thus therefore he went back, carefully looking on this side, and on that, all the way as he went, if happily he might find his roll, that had been his comfort so many times in his journey. He went thus, till he came again within sight of the arbour where he sat and slept; but that sight renewed his sorrow the more, by bringing again, even afresh, his evil of sleeping into his mind.[75] Thus, therefore, he now went on bewailing his sinful sleep, saying, "O wretched man that I am!" that I should sleep in the day time! that I should sleep in the midst of difficulty! that I should so indulge the flesh, as to use that rest for ease to my flesh, which the Lord of the hill hath erected only for the relief of the spirits of pilgrims!

How many steps have I took in vain! Thus it happened to Israel, for their sin; they were sent back again by the way of the Red Sea; and I am made to tread those steps with sorrow, which I might have trod with delight, had it not been for this sinful sleep. How far might I have been on my way by this time! I am made to tread those steps thrice over, which I needed not to have trod but once; yea, now also I am like to be benighted, for the day is almost spent. O that I had not slept!

Now by this time he was come to the arbour again, where for a while he sat down and wept; but at last, as Christian would have it, looking sorrowfully down under the settle, there he espied his roll; the which he, with trembling and haste, catched up, and put it into his bosom. But who can tell how joyful this man was when he had gotten his roll again! for this roll was the assurance of his life and acceptance at the desired haven. Therefore he laid it up in his bosom, gave thanks to God for directing his eye to the place where it lay, and with joy and tears betook himself again to his journey. But O how nimbly now did he go up the rest of the hill! Yet, before be got up, the sun went down upon Christian; and this made him again recall the vanity of his sleeping to his remembrance; and thus he again began to condole with himself. O thou sinful sleep! how, for thy sake am I like to be benighted in my journey! I must walk without the sun; darkness must cover the path of my feet;

75 Rev. 2:5; 1 Thess. 5:7, 8

and I must hear the noise of the doleful creatures, because of my sinful sleep.[76] Now also he remembered the story that Mistrust and Timorous told him of, how they were frighted with the sight of the lions. Then said Christian to himself again, These beasts range in the night for their prey; and if they should meet with me in the dark, how should I shift them? How should I escape being by them torn in pieces? Thus he went on his way. But while he was thus bewailing his unhappy miscarriage, he lift up his eyes, and behold there was a very stately palace before him, the name of which was Beautiful; and it stood just by the highway side.

So I saw in my dream, that he made haste and went forward, that if possible he might get lodging there. Now before he had gone far, he entered into a very narrow passage, which was about a furlong off of the porter's lodge; and looking very narrowly before him as he went, he espied two lions in the way. Now, thought he, I see the dangers that Mistrust and Timorous were driven back by. (The lions were chained, but he saw not the chains). Then he was afraid, and thought also himself to go back after them, for he thought nothing but death was before him. But the porter at the lodge, whose name is Watchful, perceiving that Christian made a halt as if he would go back, cried unto him, saying, Is thy strength so small?[77] Fear not the lions, for they are chained, and are placed there for trial of faith where it is, and for discovery of those that have none. Keep in the midst of the path, and no hurt shall come unto thee.

Then I saw that he went on, trembling for fear of the lions, but taking good heed to the directions of the porter; he heard them roar, but they did him no harm. Then he clapped his hands, and went on till he came and stood

76 1 Thess. 5:6, 7

77 Mark 13:34–37

before the gate, where the porter was. Then said Christian to the porter, Sir, what house is this? and may I lodge here tonight? The porter answered, This house was built by the Lord of the hill, and He built it for the relief and security of pilgrims. The porter also asked whence he was, and whither he was going.

CHRISTIAN. I am come from the City of Destruction, and am going to Mount Zion; but because the sun is now set, I desire, if I may, to lodge here tonight.

PORTER. What is your name?

CHRISTIAN. My name is now Christian, but my name at the first was Graceless; I came of the race of Japheth, whom God will persuade to dwell in the tents of Shem.[78]

PORTER. But how doth it happen that you come so late? The sun is set.

CHRISTIAN. I had been here sooner, but that, "wretched man that I am!" I slept in the arbour that stands on the hill side; nay, I had, notwithstanding that, been here much sooner, but that, in my sleep, I lost my evidence, and came without it to the brow of the hill; and then feeling for it, and finding it not, I was forced, with sorrow of heart, to go back to the place where I slept my sleep, where I found it, and now I am come.

PORTER. Well, I will call out one of the virgins of this place, who will, if she likes your talk, bring you in to the rest of the family, according to the rules of the house. So Watchful, the porter, rang a bell, at the sound of which came out at the door of the house, a grave and beautiful damsel, named Discretion, and asked why she was called.

The porter answered, This man is in a journey from the City of Destruction to Mount Zion, but being weary and benighted, he asked me if he might lodge here tonight; so I

78 Gen. 9:27

told him I would call for thee, who, after discourse had with him, mayest do as seemeth thee good, even according to the law of the house.

Then she asked him whence he was, and whither he was going; and he told her. She asked him also how he got into the way; and he told her. Then she asked him what he had seen and met with in the way; and he told her. And last she asked his name; so he said, It is Christian, and I have so much the more a desire to lodge here tonight, because, by what I perceive, this place was built by the Lord of the hill, for the relief and security of pilgrims. So she smiled, but the water stood in her eyes; and after a little pause, she said, I will call forth two or three more of the family. So she ran to the door, and called out Prudence, Piety, and Charity, who, after a little more discourse with him, had him into the family; and many of them meeting him at the threshold of the house, said, "Come in, thou blessed of the Lord"; this house was built by the Lord of the hill, on purpose to entertain such pilgrims in. Then he bowed his head, and followed them into the house. So when he was come in and sat down, they gave him something to drink, and consented together, that until supper was ready, some of them should have some particular discourse with Christian, for the best improvement of time; and they appointed Piety, and Prudence, and Charity to discourse with him; and thus they began:

PIETY. Come, good Christian, since we have been so loving to you, to receive you into our house this night, let us, if perhaps we may better ourselves thereby, talk with you of all things that have happened to you in your pilgrimage.

CHRISTIAN. With a very good will, and I am glad that you are so well disposed.

PIETY. What moved you at first to betake yourself to a pilgrim's life?

CHRISTIAN. I was driven out of my native country, by a

dreadful sound that was in mine ears; to wit, that unavoidable destruction did attend me, if I abode in that country place where I was.

PIETY. But how did it happen that you came out of your country this way?

CHRISTIAN. It was as God would have it; for when I was under the fears of destruction, I did not know whither to go; but by chance there came a man, even to me, as I was trembling and weeping, whose name is Evangelist, and he directed me to the wicket-gate, which else I should never have found, and so set me into the way that hath led me directly to this house.

PIETY. But did you not come by the house of the Interpreter?

CHRISTIAN. Yes, and did see such things there, the remembrance of which will stick by me as long as I live; especially three things, to wit, how Christ, in despite of Satan, maintains His work of grace in the heart; how the man had sinned himself quite out of hopes of God's mercy; and also the dream of him that thought in his sleep the day of judgment was come.

PIETY. Why, did you hear him tell his dream?

CHRISTIAN. Yes, and a dreadful one it was. I thought it made my heart ache as he was telling of it; but yet I am glad I heard it.

PIETY. Was that all that you saw at the house of the Interpreter?

CHRISTIAN. No; he took me and had me where he showed me a stately palace, and how the people were clad in gold that were in it; and how there came a venturous man and cut his way through the armed men that stood in the door to keep him out; and how he was bid to come in, and win eternal glory. Methought those things did ravish my heart! I would have staid at that good man's house a twelvemonth, but that I knew I had further to go.

PIETY. And what saw you else in the way?

CHRISTIAN. Saw! why, I went but a little further, and I saw one, as I thought in my mind, hang bleeding upon the tree; and the very sight of Him made my burden fall off my back (for I groaned under a very heavy burden), but then it fell down from off me. It was a strange thing to me, for I never saw such a thing before; yea, and while I stood looking up, for then I could not forbear looking, three Shining Ones came to me. One of them testified that my sins were forgiven me; another stripped me of my rags, and gave me this broidered coat which you see; and the third set the mark which you see in my forehead, and gave me this sealed roll. (And with that he plucked it out of his bosom).

PIETY. But you saw more than this, did you not?

CHRISTIAN. The things that I have told you were the best, yet some other matters I saw, as, namely, I saw three men, Simple, Sloth, and Presumption, lie asleep a little out of the way, as I came, with irons upon their heels; but do you think I could awake them? I also saw Formality and Hypocrisy come tumbling over the wall, to go, as they pretended, to Zion, but they were quickly lost, even as I myself did tell them; but they would not believe. But above all, I found it hard work to get up this hill, and as hard to come by the lions' mouths; and truly if it had not been for the good man, the porter that stands at the gate, I do not know but that after all I might have gone back again; but now, I thank God I am here, and I thank you for receiving of me.

Then Prudence thought good to ask him a few questions, and desired his answer to them.

PRUDENCE. Do you not think sometimes of the country from whence you came?

CHRISTIAN. Yes, but with much shame and detestation:

"truly if I had been mindful of that country from whence I came out, I might have had opportunity to have returned; but now I desire a better country, that is, an heavenly"[79]

PRUDENCE. Do you not yet bear away with you some of the things that then you were conversant withal?

CHRISTIAN. Yes, but greatly against my will; especially my inward and carnal cogitations, with which all my countrymen, as well as myself, were delighted; but now all those things are my grief; and might I but choose mine own things, I would choose never to think of those things more; but when I would be doing of that which is best, that which is worst is with me.[80]

PRUDENCE. Do you not find sometimes, as if those things were vanquished, which at other times are your perplexity?

CHRISTIAN. Yes, but that is but seldom; but they are to me golden hours, in which such things happen to me.

PRUDENCE. Can you remember by what means you find your annoyances, at times, as if they were vanquished?

CHRISTIAN. Yes; when I think what I saw at the cross, that will do it; and when I look upon my broidered coat, that will do it; also when I look into the roll that I carry in my bosom, that will do it; and when my thoughts wax warm about whither I am going, that will do it.

PRUDENCE. And what is it that makes you so desirous to go to Mount Zion?

CHRISTIAN. Why, there I hope to see Him alive that did hang dead on the cross; and there I hope to be rid of all those things that to this day are in me an annoyance to me; there, they say, there is no death; and there I shall dwell with

79 Heb. 11:15, 16

80 Rom. 7

such company as I like best.[81] For, to tell you truth, I love Him, because I was by Him eased of my burden; and I am weary of my inward sickness. I would fain be where I shall die no more, and with the company that shall continually cry, "Holy, holy, holy."

Then said Charity to Christian, Have you a family? Are you a married man?

CHRISTIAN. I have a wife and four small children.

CHARITY. And why did you not bring them along with you?

CHRISTIAN. Then Christian wept, and said, O how willingly would I have done it! but they were all of them utterly averse to my going on pilgrimage.

CHARITY. But you should have talked to them, and have endeavoured to have shown them the danger of being behind.

CHRISTIAN. So I did; and told them also what God had shown to me of the destruction of our city; "but I seemed to them as one that mocked," and they believed me not (Gen. 19:14).

CHARITY. And did you pray to God that He would bless your counsel to them?

CHRISTIAN. Yes, and that with much affection; for you must think that my wife and poor children were very dear unto me.

CHARITY. But did you tell them of your own sorrow, and fear of destruction? for I suppose that destruction was visible enough to you.

CHRISTIAN. Yes, over, and over, and over. They might also see my fears in my countenance, in my tears, and also in my trembling under the apprehension of the judgment that

81 Isa. 25:8; Rev. 21:4

did hang over our heads; but all was not sufficient to prevail with them to come with me.

CHARITY. But what could they say for themselves, why they came not?

CHRISTIAN. Why, my wife was afraid of losing this world, and my children were given to the foolish delights of youth; so what by one thing, and what by another, they left me to wander in this manner alone.

CHARITY. But did you not, with your vain life, damp all that you by words used by way of persuasion to bring them away with you?

CHRISTIAN. Indeed, I cannot commend my life; for I am conscious to myself of many failings therein; I know also, that a man by his conversation may soon overthrow, what by argument or persuasion he doth labour to fasten upon others for their good. Yet this I can say, I was very wary of giving them occasion, by any unseemly action, to make them averse to going on pilgrimage. Yea, for this very thing, they would tell me I was too precise, and that I denied myself of things, for their sakes, in which they saw no evil. Nay, I think I may say, that if what they saw in me did hinder them, it was my great tenderness in sinning against God, or of doing any wrong to my neighbour.

CHARITY. Indeed Cain hated his brother, "because his own works were evil, and his brother's righteous"[82] and if thy wife and children have been offended with thee for this, they thereby show themselves to be implacable to good, and "thou hast delivered thy soul from their blood"[83]

Now I saw in my dream, that thus they sat talking together until supper was ready. So when they had made ready, they sat down to meat. Now the table was furnished "with

82 1 John 3:12

83 Ezek. 3:19

fat things, and with wine that was well refined": and all their talk at the table was about the Lord of the hill; as, namely, about what He had done, and wherefore He did what He did, and why He had builded that house. And by what they said, I perceived that He had been a great warrior, and had fought with and slain "him that had the power of death," but not without great danger to Himself, which made me love Him the more.[84]

For, as they said, and as I believe (said Christian), He did it with the loss of much blood; but that which put glory of grace into all He did, was, that He did it out of pure love to His country. And besides, there were some of them of the household that said they had been and spoke with Him since He did die on the cross; and they have attested that they had it from His own lips, that He is such a lover of poor pilgrims, that the like is not to be found from the east to the west.

They, moreover, gave an instance of what they affirmed, and that was, He had stripped Himself of His glory, that He might do this for the poor; and that they heard Him say and affirm, "that He would not dwell in the mountain of Zion alone." They said, moreover, that He had made many pilgrims princes, though by nature they were beggars born, and their original had been the dunghill.[85]

Thus they discoursed together till late at night; and after they had committed themselves to their Lord for protection, they betook themselves to rest: the Pilgrim they laid in a large upper chamber, whose window opened toward the sun-rising; the name of the chamber was Peace; where he slept till break of day, and then he awoke and sang—

84 Heb. 2:14, 15

85 1 Sam. 2:8; Psa. 113:7

Where am I now? Is this the love and care
Of Jesus for the men that pilgrims are?
Thus to provide! that I should be forgiven!
And dwell already the next door to Heaven!

So, in the morning, they all got up; and after some more discourse, they told him that he should not depart till they had shown him the rarities of that place. And first, they had him into the study, where they showed him records of the greatest antiquity; in which, as I remember my dream, they showed him first the pedigree of the Lord of the hill, that He was the Son of the Ancient of Days, and came by that eternal generation. Here also was more fully recorded the acts that He had done, and the names of many hundreds that He had taken into His service; and how He had placed them in such habitations, that could neither by length of days, nor decays of nature, be dissolved.

Then they read to him some of the worthy acts that some of His servants had done: as, how they had "subdued kingdoms, wrought righteousness, obtained promises, stopped the mouths of lions, quenched the violence of fire, escaped the edge of the sword, out of weakness were made strong, waxed valiant in fight, and turned to flight the armies of the aliens.[86]

They then read again in another part of the records of the house, where it was showed how willing their Lord was to receive into His favour any, even any, though they in time past had offered great affronts to His person and proceedings. Here also were several other histories of many other famous things, of all which Christian had a view; as of things both ancient and modern; together with prophecies and predictions of things that have their certain accomplish-

86 Heb. 11:33, 34

ment, both to the dread and amazement of enemies, and the comfort and solace of pilgrims.

The next day they took him and had him into the armoury, where they showed him all manner of furniture, which their Lord had provided for pilgrims, as sword, shield, helmet, breastplate, all-prayer, and shoes that would not wear out. And there was here enough of this to harness out as many men, for the service of their Lord, as there be stars in the Heaven for multitude.

They also showed him some of the engines with which some of his servants had done wonderful things. They showed him Moses' rod; the hammer and nail with which Jael slew Sisera; the pitchers, trumpets, and lamps too, with which Gibeon put to flight the armies of Midian. Then they showed him the ox's goad wherewith Shamgar slew 600 men. They showed him, also, the jaw-bone with which Samson did such mighty feats. They showed him, moreover, the sling and stone with which David slew Goliath of Gath; and the sword, also, with which their Lord will kill the Man of Sin, in the day that he shall rise up to the prey. They showed him, besides, many excellent things, with which Christian was much delighted. This done, they went to their rest again.

Then I saw in my dream, that, on the morrow, he got up to go forward; but they desired him to stay till the next day also; and then, said they, we will, if the day be clear, show you the Delectable Mountains, which, they said, would yet further add to his comfort, because they were nearer the desired haven than the place where at present he was; so he consented and staid. When the morning was up, they had him to the top of the house, and bid him look south; so he did; and, behold, at a great distance, he saw a most pleasant mountainous country, beautified with woods, vineyards, fruits of all sorts, flowers also, with springs and fountains, very delectable to behold.[87] Then he asked the name of the country. They said it was Immanuel's Land; and it is as common, said they, as this hill is, to and for all the pilgrims. And when thou comest there, from thence, said they, thou mayest see to the gate of the Celestial City, as the shepherds that live there will make appear.

Now, he bethought himself of setting forward, and they were willing he should, But first, said they, let us go again into the armoury. So they did; and when they came there, they harnessed him from head to foot with what was of proof, lest, perhaps, he should meet with assaults in the way. He being, therefore, thus accoutred, walketh out with his friends to the gate, and there he asked the porter if he saw any pilgrims pass by. Then the porter answered, Yes.

CHRISTIAN. Pray, did you know him? said he.

PORTER. I asked his name, and he told me it was Faithful.

CHRISTIAN. O, said Christian, I know him; he is my townsman, my near neighbour; he comes from the place where I was born. How far do you think he may be before?

PORTER. He is got by this time below the hill.

CHRISTIAN. Well, said Christian, good Porter, the Lord be with thee, and add to all thy blessings much increase, for the kindness that thou hast showed to me.

87 Isa. 33:16, 17

THE VALLEY OF HUMILIATION

Then he began to go forward; but Discretion, Piety, Charity, and Prudence, would accompany him down to the foot of the hill. So they went on together, reiterating their former discourses, till they came to go down the hill. Then, said Christian, as it was difficult coming up, so, so far as I can see, it is dangerous going down. Yes, said Prudence, so it is, for it is a hard matter for a man to go down into the Valley of Humiliation, as thou art now, and to catch no slip by the way; therefore, said they, are we come out to accompany thee down the hill. So he began to go down, but very warily; yet he caught a slip or two. Then I saw in my dream that these good companions, when Christian was gone to the bottom of the hill, gave him a loaf of bread, a bottle of wine, and a cluster of raisins; and then he went on his way.

But now, in this Valley of Humiliation, poor Christian was hard put to it; for he had gone but a little way, before he espied a foul fiend coming over the field to meet him; his name is Apollyon. Then did Christian begin to be afraid, and to cast in his mind whether to go back or to stand his ground. But he considered again that he had no armour for his back; and, therefore, thought that to turn the back to him might give him the greater advantage, with ease to pierce him with his darts. Therefore he resolved to venture and stand his ground; for, thought he, had I no more in mine eye than the saving of my life, it would be the best way to stand.

So he went on, and Apollyon met him. Now the monster was hideous to behold; he was clothed with scales, like a fish (and they are his pride), he had wings like a dragon, feet like a bear, and out of his belly came fire and smoke, and his mouth was as the mouth of a lion. When he was come up to Christian, he beheld him with a disdainful countenance, and thus began to question with him.

APOLLYON. Whence come you? and whither are you bound?

CHRISTIAN. I am come from the City of Destruction, which is the place of all evil, and am going to the City of Zion.

APOLLYON. By this I perceive thou art one of my subjects, for all that country is mine, and I am the prince and god of it. How is it, then, that thou hast run away from thy king? Were it not that I hope thou mayest do me more service, I would strike thee now, at one blow, to the ground.

CHRISTIAN. I was born, indeed, in your dominions, but your service was hard, and your wages such as a man could not live on, "for the wages of sin is death";[88] therefore, when I was come to years, I did as other considerate persons do, look out, if, perhaps, I might mend myself.

APOLLYON. There is no prince that will thus lightly lose his subjects, neither will I as yet lose thee; but since thou complainest of thy service and wages, be content to go back; what our country will afford, I do here promise to give thee.

CHRISTIAN. But I have let myself to another, even to the King of princes; and how can I, with fairness, go back with thee?

APOLLYON. Thou hast done in this according to the

88 Rom. 6:23

proverb, "Changed a bad for a worse"; but it is ordinary for those that have professed themselves His servants, after a while to give Him the slip, and return again to me. Do thou so too, and all shall be well.

CHRISTIAN. I have given Him my faith, and sworn my allegiance to Him; how, then, can I go back from this, and not be hanged as a traitor?

APOLLYON. Thou didst the same to me, and yet I am willing to pass by all, if now thou wilt yet turn again and go back.

CHRISTIAN. What I promised thee was in my nonage; and, besides, I count the Prince under whose banner now I stand is able to absolve me; yea, and to pardon also what I did as to my compliance with thee; and besides, O thou destroying Apollyon! to speak truth, I like His service, His wages, His servants, His government, His company, and country, better than thine; and, therefore, leave off to persuade me further; I am His servant, and I will follow Him.

APOLLYON. Consider again, when thou art in cool blood, what thou art like to meet with in the way that thou goest. Thou knowest that, for the most part, His servants come to an ill end, because they are transgressors against me and my ways. How many of them have been put to shameful deaths! and, besides, thou countest His service better than mine, whereas He never came yet from the place where He is to deliver any that served Him out of their hands; but as for me, how many times, as all the world very well knows, have I delivered, either by power or fraud, those that have faithfully served me, from Him and His, though taken by them; and so I will deliver thee.

CHRISTIAN. His forbearing at present to deliver them is on purpose to try their love, whether they will cleave to Him to the end; and as for the ill end thou sayest they come to, that is most glorious in their account; for, for present deliverance, they do not much expect it, for they stay for their glory, and then they shall have it, when their Prince comes in His and the glory of the angels.

APOLLYON. Thou hast already been unfaithful in thy service to Him; and how dost thou think to receive wages of Him?

CHRISTIAN. Wherein, O Apollyon! have I been unfaithful to Him?

APOLLYON. Thou didst faint at first setting out, when thou wast almost choked in the Gulf of Despond; thou didst attempt wrong ways to be rid of thy burden, whereas against thou shouldest have stayed till thy Prince had taken it off; thou didst sinfully sleep, and lose thy choice thing; thou wast, also, almost persuaded to go back, at the sight of the lions; and when thou talkest of thy journey, and of what thou hast heard and seen, thou art inwardly desirous of vain-glory in all that thou sayest or doest.

CHRISTIAN. All this is true, and much more which thou has left out; but the Prince, whom I serve and honour, is merciful, and ready to forgive; but, besides, these infirmities possessed me in thy country, for there I sucked them in; and I have groaned under them, been sorry for them, and have obtained pardon of my Prince.

COMBAT WITH APPOLYON

APOLLYON. Then Apollyon broke out into a grievous rage, saying, I am an enemy to this Prince; I hate His person, His laws, and people; I am come out on purpose to withstand thee.

CHRISTIAN. Apollyon, beware what you do; for I am in the king's highway, the way of holiness; therefore take heed to yourself.

APOLLYON. Then Apollyon straddled quite over the whole breadth of the way, and said, I am void of fear in this matter: prepare thyself to die; for I swear by my infernal den, that thou shalt go no further; here will I spill thy soul.

And with that he threw a flaming dart at his breast; but Christian had a shield in his hand, with which he caught it, and so prevented the danger of that.

Then did Christian draw; for he saw it was time to bestir him: and Apollyon as fast made at him, throwing darts as thick as hail; by the which, notwithstanding all that Christian could do to avoid it, Apollyon wounded him in his head, his hand, and foot. This made Christian give a little back; Apollyon, therefore, followed his work amain, and Christian again took courage, and resisted as manfully as he could. This sore combat lasted for above half a day, even till Christian was almost quite spent; for you must know, that

Christian, by reason of his wounds, must needs grow weaker and weaker.

Then Apollyon, espying his opportunity, began to gather up close to Christian, and wrestling with him, gave him a dreadful fall; and with that, Christian's sword flew out of his hand. Then said Apollyon, I am sure of thee now. And with that he had almost pressed him to death; so that Christian began to despair of life: but as God would have it, while Apollyon was fetching of his last blow, thereby to make a full end of this good man, Christian nimbly stretched out his hand for his sword, and caught it, saying, "Rejoice not against me, O mine enemy: when I fall, I shall arise"[89]; and with that gave him a deadly thrust, which made him give back, as one that had received his mortal wound. Christian perceiving that, made at him again, saying, "Nay, in all these things we are more than conquerors, through Him that loved us"[90] And with that Apollyon spread forth his dragon's wings, and sped him away, that Christian for a season saw him no more.[91]

In this combat no man can imagine, unless he had seen and heard as I did, what yelling and hideous roaring Apollyon made all the time of the fight—he spake like a dragon; and, on the other side, what sighs and groans burst from Christian's heart. I never saw him all the while give so much as one pleasant look, till he perceived he had wounded Apollyon with his two-edged sword; then, indeed, he did smile, and look upward; but it was the most dreadful sight that ever I saw.

So when the battle was over, Christian said, "I will here give thanks to Him that delivered me out of the mouth of

89 Micah. 7:8

90 Rom. 8:37

91 James 4:7

the lion, to Him that did help me against Apollyon." And so he did, saying—

Great Beelzebub, the captain of this fiend,
Design'd my ruin; therefore to this end
He sent him harness'd out; and he with rage,
That hellish was, did fiercely me engage.
But blessed Michael helped me, and I,
By dint of sword, did quickly make him fly.
Therefore to him let me give lasting praise,
And thank and bless his holy name always.

Then there came to him a hand, with some of the leaves of the tree of life, the which Christian took, and applied to the wounds that he had received in the battle, and was healed immediately. He also sat down in that place to eat bread, and to drink of the bottle that was given him a little before; so being refreshed, he addressed himself to his journey, with his sword drawn in his hand; for he said, I know not but some other enemy may be at hand. But he met with no other affront from Apollyon quite through this valley.

Now, at the end of this valley, was another, The Valley of the Shadow of Death. and Christian must needs go through it, because the way to the Celestial City lay through the midst of it. Now this valley is a very solitary place. The prophet Jeremiah thus describes it: "A wilderness, a land of deserts, and of pits, a land of drought, and of the shadow of death, a land that no man" (but a Christian) "passed through, and where no man dwelt"[92].

Now here Christian was worse put to it than in his fight with Apollyon; as by the sequel you shall see.

I saw then in my dream, that when Christian was got

92 Jer. 2:6

to the borders of the Shadow of Death, there met him two men, children of them that brought up an evil report of the good land,[93] making haste to go back; to whom Christian spake as follows—

CHRISTIAN. Whither are you going?

MEN. They said, Back! back! and we would have you to do so too, if either life or peace is prized by you.

CHRISTIAN. Why? what's the matter? said Christian.

MEN. Matter! said they; we were going that way as you are going, and went as far as we durst; and indeed we were almost past coming back; for had we gone a little further, we had not been here to bring the news to thee.

CHRISTIAN. But what have you met with? said Christian.

MEN. Why, we were almost in the Valley of the Shadow of Death; but that, by good hap, we looked before us, and saw the danger before we came to it.[94]

CHRISTIAN. But what have you seen? said Christian.

MEN. Seen! Why, the valley itself, which is as dark as pitch; we also saw there the hobgoblins, satyrs, and dragons of the pit; we heard also in that Valley a continual howling and yelling, as of a people under unutterable misery, who there sat bound in affliction and irons; and over that Valley hangs the discouraging clouds of confusion. Death also doth always spread his wings over it. In a word, it is every whit dreadful, being utterly without order.[95]

CHRISTIAN. Then said Christian, I perceive not yet, by what you have said, but that this is my way to the desired haven.[96]

93 Num. 13

94 Psa. 44:19; 107:10

95 Job 3:5; 10:22

96 Jer. 2:6

MEN. Be it thy way; we will not choose it for ours. So they parted, and Christian went on his way, but still with his sword drawn in his hand; for fear lest he should be assaulted.

I saw then in my dream so far as this valley reached, there was on the right hand a very deep ditch: that ditch is it into which the blind have led the blind in all ages, and have both there miserably perished.[97] Again, behold, on the left hand, there was a very dangerous quag, into which, if even a good man falls, he can find no bottom for his foot to stand on. Into that quag king David once did fall, and had no doubt therein been smothered, had not HE that is able plucked him out.

The pathway was here also exceeding narrow, and therefore good Christian was the more put to it; for when he sought, in the dark, to shun the ditch on the one hand, he was ready to tip over into the mire on the other; also when he sought to escape the mire, without great carefulness he would be ready to fall into the ditch. Thus he went on, and I heard him here sigh bitterly; for besides the dangers mentioned above, the pathway was here so dark, that ofttimes, when he lift up his foot to set forward, he knew not where, or upon what he should set it next.

About the midst of this valley, I perceived the mouth of hell to be, and it stood also hard by the way-side. Now, thought Christian, what shall I do? And ever and anon the flame and smoke would come out in such abundance, with sparks and hideous noises (things that cared not for Christian's sword, as did Apollyon before), that he was forced to put up his sword, and betake himself to another weapon, called All-prayer.[98] So he cried in my hearing, "O Lord, I

97 Psa. 69:14, 15
98 Eph. 4:18

beseech Thee, deliver my soul!".[99] Thus he went on a great while, yet still the flames would be reaching towards him. Also he heard doleful voices, and rushings to and fro, so that sometimes he thought he should be torn in pieces, or trodden down like mire in the streets. This frightful sight was seen, and these dreadful noises were heard by him for several miles together. And, coming to a place, where he thought he heard a company of fiends coming forward to meet him, he stopped and began to muse what he had best to do. Sometimes he had half a thought to go back; then again he thought he might be half way through the valley; he remembered also how he had already vanquished many a danger, and that the danger of going back might be much more than for to go forward; so he resolved to go on. Yet the fiends seemed to come nearer and nearer; but when they were come even almost at him, he cried out with a most vehement voice, "I will walk in the strength of the Lord God"; so they gave back, and came no further.

One thing I would not let slip; I took notice that now poor Christian was so confounded, that he did not know his own voice; and thus I perceived it. Just when he was come over against the mouth of the burning pit, one of the wicked ones got behind him, and stept up softly to him, and, whisperingly, suggested many grievous blasphemies to him, which he verily thought had proceeded from his own mind. This put Christian more to it than anything that he met with before; even to think that he should now blaspheme Him that he loved so much before; yet, if he could have helped it, he would not have done it; but he had not the discretion either to stop his ears, or to know from whence these blasphemies came.

When Christian had traveled in this disconsolate con-

99 Psa. 116:4

dition some considerable time, he thought he heard the voice of a man, as going before him, saying, "Though I walk through the valley of the shadow of death, I will fear no evil; for Thou art with me".[100]

Then he was glad, and that for these reasons:

First, Because he gathered from thence, that some who feared God, were in this valley as well as himself.

Secondly, For that he perceived God was with them, though in that dark and dismal state; and why not, thought he, with me? though, by reason of the impediment that attends this place, I cannot perceive it.[101]

Thirdly, For that he hoped, could he overtake them, to have company by and by. So he went on, and called to him that was before; but he knew not what to answer; for that he also thought himself to be alone. And by and by the day broke; then said Christian, He hath turned "the shadow of death into the morning".[102]

Now morning being come, he looked back, not out of desire to return, but to see, by the light of the day, what hazards he had gone through in the dark. So he saw more perfectly the ditch that was on the one hand, and the quag that was on the other; also how narrow the way was which led betwixt them both; also now he saw the hobgoblins, and satyrs, and dragons of the pit, but all afar off (for after break of day, they came not nigh); yet they were discovered to him, according to that which is written, "He discovereth deep things out of darkness, and bringeth out to light the shadow of death".[103]

Now was Christian much affected with his deliverance

100 Psa. 23:4

101 Job. 9:11

102 Amos 5:8

103 Job 12:22

from all the dangers of his solitary way; which dangers, though he feared them more before, yet he saw them more clearly now, because the light of the day made them conspicuous to him. And about this time the sun was rising, and this was another mercy to Christian; for you must note, that though the first part of the Valley of the Shadow of Death was dangerous, yet this second part which he was yet to go, was, if possible, far more dangerous: for from the place where he now stood, even to the end of the valley, the way was all along set so full of snares, traps, gins, and nets here, and so full of pits, pitfalls, deep holes, and shelvings down there, that had it now been dark, as it were when he came the first part of the way, had he had a thousand souls, they had in reason been cast away; but, as I said, just now the sun was rising. Then said he, "His candle shineth upon my head, and by His light I walk through darkness".[104]

In this light, therefore, he came to the end of the valley. Now I saw in my dream, that at the end of this valley lay blood, bones, ashes, and mangled bodies of men, even of pilgrims that had gone this way formerly; and while I was musing what should be the reason, I espied a little before me a cave, where two giants, POPE and PAGAN, dwelt in old time; by whose power and tyranny the men whose bones, blood, ashes, etc., lay there, were cruelly put to death. But by this place Christian went without much danger, whereat I somewhat wondered; but I have learnt since, that PAGAN has been dead many a day; and as for the other, though he be yet alive, he is, by reason of age, and also of the many shrewd brushes that he met with in his younger days, grown so crazy and stiff in his joints, that he can now do little more than sit in his cave's mouth, grinning at pilgrims as they go by, and biting his nails because he cannot come at them.

104 Job 29:3

So I saw that Christian went on his way; yet, at the sight of the Old Man that sat in the mouth of the cave, he could not tell what to think, especially because he spake to him, though he could not go after him; saying, "You will never mend, till more of you be burned." But he held his peace, and set a good face on it, and so went by and catched no hurt. Then sang Christian,

O world of wonders! (I can say no less)
That I should be preserv'd in that distress
That I have met with here! O blessed be
That hand that from it hath deliver'd me!
Dangers in darkness, devils, hell, and sin,
Did compass me, while I this vale was in:
Yea, snares and pits, and traps, and nets, did lie
My path about, that worthless, silly I
Might have been catch'd, entangled, and cast down;
But since I live, let JESUS wear the crown.

Now, as Christian went on his way, he came to a little ascent, which was cast up on purpose, that pilgrims might see before them. Up there, therefore, Christian went; and looking forward, he saw Faithful before him, upon his journey. Then said Christian aloud, "Ho! ho! Soho! stay, and I will be your companion." At that, Faithful looked behind him; to whom Christian cried again, "Stay, stay, till I come up to you." But Faithful answered, "No, I am upon my life, and the avenger of blood is behind me."

CHRISTIAN OVERTAKES FAITHFUL

At this, Christian was somewhat moved, and putting to all his strength, he quickly got up with Faithful, and did also overrun him; so the last was first. Then did Christian vain-gloriously smile, because he had gotten the start of his brother; but not taking good heed to his feet, he suddenly stumbled and fell, and could not rise again, until Faithful came up to help him.

Then I saw in my dream, they went very lovingly on together, and had sweet discourse of all things that had happened to them in their pilgrimage; and thus Christian began.

CHRISTIAN. My honoured and well-beloved brother, Faithful, I am glad that I have overtaken you; and that God has so tempered our spirits, that we can walk as companions in this so pleasant a path.

FAITHFUL. I had thought, dear friend, to have had your company quite from our town; but you did get the start of me, wherefore I was forced to come thus much of the way alone.

CHRISTIAN. How long did you stay in the City of Destruction, before you set out after me on your pilgrimage

FAITHFUL. Till I could stay no longer; for there was great talk presently after you were gone out, that our city would, in short time, with fire from Heaven, be burned down to the ground.

CHRISTIAN. What! did your neighbours talk so?

FAITHFUL. Yes, it was for a while in everybody's mouth.

CHRISTIAN. What! and did no more of them but you come out to escape the danger?

FAITHFUL. Though there were, as I said, a great talk thereabout, yet I do not think they did firmly believe it. For in the heat of the discourse, I heard some of them deridingly speak of you, and of your desperate journey (for so they called this your pilgrimage), but I did believe, and do still, that the end of our city will be with fire and brimstone from above; and therefore I have made my escape.

CHRISTIAN. Did you hear no talk of neighbour Pliable?

FAITHFUL. Yes, Christian, I heard that he followed you till he came at the Slough of Despond, where, as some said, he fell in; but he would not be known to have so done; but I am sure he was soundly bedabbled with that kind of dirt.

CHRISTIAN. And what said the neighbours to him?

FAITHFUL. He hath, since his going back, been had greatly in derision, and that among all sorts of people; some do mock and despise him; and scarce will any set him on work. He is now seven times worse than if he had never gone out of the City.

CHRISTIAN. But why should they be so set against him, since they also despise the way that he forsook?

FAITHFUL. O! they say, Hang him, he is a turn-coat; he was not true to his profession. I think God has stirred up even his enemies to hiss at him, and make him a proverb, because he hath forsaken the way.[105]

CHRISTIAN. Had you no talk with him before you came out?

105 Jer. 29:18, 19

FAITHFUL. I met him once in the streets, but be leered away on the other side, as one ashamed of what he had done; so I spake not to him.

CHRISTIAN. Well, at my first setting out, I had hopes of that man; but now I fear he will perish in the overthrow of the city; For it is happened to him according to the true proverb, The dog is turned to his own vomit again; and the sow that was washed, to her wallowing in the mire".[106]

FAITHFUL. These are my fears of him too; but who can hinder that which will be?

CHRISTIAN. Well, neighbour Faithful, said Christian, let us leave him, and talk of things that more immediately concern ourselves. Tell me now, what you have met with in the way as you came; for I know you have met with some things, or else it may be writ for a wonder.

FAITHFUL. I escaped the Slough that I perceived you fell into, and got up to the gate without that danger; only I met with one whose name was Wanton, who had like to have done me a mischief.

CHRISTIAN. It was well you escaped her net; Joseph was hard put to it by her, and he escaped her as you did; but it had like to have cost him his life.[107] But what did she do to you?

FAITHFUL. You cannot think, but that you know something, what a flattering tongue she had; she lay at me hard to turn aside with her, promising me all manner of content.

CHRISTIAN. Nay, she did not promise you the content of a good conscience.

FAITHFUL. You know what I mean; all carnal and fleshly content.

106 2 Peter 2:22

107 Gen. 39:11–13

CHRISTIAN. Thank God you have escaped her; "the abhorred of the Lord shall fall into her ditch" (Pro. 22:14).

FAITHFUL. Nay, I know not whether I did wholly escape her or no.

CHRISTIAN. Why, I trow you did not consent to her desires?

FAITHFUL. No, not to defile myself; for I remembered an old writing that I had seen, which said, "Her steps take hold on hell".[108] So I shut mine eyes, because I would not be bewitched with her looks.[109] Then she railed on me, and I went my way.

CHRISTIAN. Did you meet with no other assault as you came?

FAITHFUL. When I came to the foot of the hill called Difficulty, I met with a very aged man, who asked me what I was, and whither bound. I told him that I am a pilgrim, going to the Celestial City. Then said the old man, Thou lookest like an honest fellow; wilt thou be content to dwell with me for the wages that I shall give thee? Then I asked him his name, and where he dwelt. He said his name was Adam the First, and that he dwelt in the town of Deceit.[110] I asked him then, what was his work, and what the wages that he would give. He told me, that his work was many delights; and his wages, that I should be his heir at last. I further asked him, what house he kept, and what other servants he had. So he told me, that his house was maintained with all the dainties in the world; and that his servants were those of his own begetting. Then I asked if he had any children. He said that he had but three daughters; the Lust of the Flesh, the Lust of the Eyes, and the Pride of Life, and that I should

108 Prov. 5:5
109 Job 31:1
110 Eph. 4:22

marry them all if I would.[111] Then I asked how long time he would have me live with him? And he told me, As long as he lived himself.

CHRISTIAN. Well, and what conclusion came the old man and you to, at last?

FAITHFUL. Why, at first, I found myself somewhat inclinable to go with the man, for I thought he spake very fair; but looking in his forehead, as I talked with him, I saw there written, "Put off the old man with his deeds."

CHRISTIAN. And how then?

FAITHFUL. Then it came burning hot into my mind, whatever he said, and however he flattered, when he got me home to his house, he would sell me for a slave. So I bid him forbear to talk, for I would not come near the door of his house. Then he reviled me, and told me, that he would send such a one after me, that should make my way bitter to my soul. So I turned to go away from him; but just as I turned myself to go thence, I felt him take hold of my flesh, and give me such a deadly twitch back, that I thought he had pulled part of me after himself. This made me cry, "O wretched man!".[112] So I went on my way up the hill.

Now when I had got about half way up, I looked behind, and saw one coming after me, swift as the wind; so he overtook me just about the place where the settle stands.

CHRISTIAN. Just there, said Christian, did I sit down to rest me; but being overcome with sleep, I there lost this roll out of my bosom

FAITHFUL. But, good brother, hear me out. So soon as the man overtook me, he was but a word and a blow, for down he knocked me, and laid me for dead. But when I was a little come to myself again, I asked him wherefore

111 1 John 2:16

112 Rom. 7:24

he served me so. He said, because of my secret inclining to Adam the First: and with that he struck me another deadly blow on the breast, and beat me down backward; so I lay at his foot as dead as before. So, when I came to myself again, I cried him mercy; but he said, I know not how to show mercy; and with that knocked me down again. He had doubtless made an end of me, but that One came by, and bid him forbear.

CHRISTIAN. Who was that that bid him forbear.

FAITHFUL. I did not know Him at first, but as He went by, I perceived the holes in His hands, and in His side; then I concluded that He was our Lord. So I went up the hill.

CHRISTIAN. That man that overtook you was Moses. He spareth none, neither knoweth he how to show mercy to those that transgress his law.

FAITHFUL. I know it very well; it was not the first time that he has met with me. It was he that came to me when I dwelt securely at home, and that told me he would burn my house over my head, if I stayed there.

CHRISTIAN. But did you not see the house that stood there on the top of the hill, on the side of which Moses met you?

FAITHFUL. Yes, and the lions too, before I came at it; but for the lions, I think they were asleep; for it was about noon; and because I had so much of the day before me, I passed by the porter, and came down the hill.

CHRISTIAN. He told me indeed, that he saw you go by, but I wish you had called at the house, for they would have showed you so many rarities, that you would scarce have forgot them to the day of your death. But pray tell me, Did you meet nobody in the Valley of Humility?

FAITHFUL. Yes, I met with one Discontent, who would willingly have persuaded me to go back again with him; his reason was, for that the valley was altogether without honour. He told me, moreover, that there to go was the way to disobey all my friends, as Pride, Arrogancy, Self-conceit, Worldly-glory, with others, who, he knew, as he said, would be very much offended, if I made such a fool of myself as to wade through this valley.

CHRISTIAN. Well, and how did you answer him?

FAITHFUL. I told him that although all these that he named might claim kindred of me, and that rightly, for indeed they were my relations according to the flesh, yet since I became a pilgrim, they have disowned me, as I also have rejected them; and therefore they were to me now no more than if they had never been of my lineage.

I told him, moreover, that as to this valley he had quite misrepresented the thing; "for before honour is humility; and a haughty spirit before a fall." Therefore, said I, I had rather go through this valley to the honour that was so accounted by the wisest, than choose that which he esteemed most worthy our affections.

CHRISTIAN. Met you with nothing else in that valley?

FAITHFUL. Yes, I met with Shame; but of all the men that I met with in my pilgrimage, he, I think, bears the wrong name. The others would be said nay, after a little argumentation, and somewhat else; but this bold-faced Shame would never have done.

CHRISTIAN. Why, what did he say to you?

FAITHFUL. What! why, he objected against religion itself; he said it was a pitiful, low, sneaking business for a man to mind religion; he said that a tender conscience was an unmanly thing; and that for a man to watch over his words and ways, so as to tie up himself from that hectoring liberty, that the brave spirits of the times accustom themselves unto, would make him the ridicule of the times. He objected also, that but few of the mighty, rich, or wise, were ever of my opinion;[113] nor any of them neither,[114] before they were persuaded to be fools, and to be of a voluntary fondness, to venture the loss of all, for nobody knows what. He moreover objected the base and low estate and condition of those that were chiefly the pilgrims, of the times in which they lived; also their ignorance, and want of understanding in all natural science. Yea, he did hold me to it at that rate also, about a great many more things than here I relate; as, that it was a shame to sit whining and mourning under a sermon, and a shame to come sighing and groaning home; that it was a shame to ask my neighbour forgiveness for petty faults, or to make restitution where I have taken from any. He said also, that religion made a man grow strange to the great, because of a few vices, which he called by finer names; and made him own and respect the base, because of the same religious fraternity. And is not this, said he, a shame?

CHRISTIAN. And what did you say to him?

FAITHFUL. Say! I could not tell what to say at the first. Yea, he put me so to it, that my blood came up in my face; even this Shame fetched it up, and had almost beat me quite off. But, at last, I began to consider, that "that which is highly esteemed among men, is had in abomination with God".[115] And I thought again, this Shame tells me what men are; but it tells me nothing what God, or the Word of God is. And I thought, moreover, that at the day of doom, we shall not be doomed to death or life, according to the hectoring spirits of the world, but according to the wisdom and law of the Highest. Therefore, thought I, what God says is best, indeed is best, though all the men in the world are against it. Seeing, then, that God prefers His religion; seeing God prefers

113 1 Cor. 1:26; 3:18; Phil. 3:7, 8

114 John 7:48

115 Luke 16:15

a tender conscience; seeing they that make themselves fools for the kingdom of Heaven are wisest; and that the poor man that loveth Christ is richer than the greatest man in the world that hates Him; Shame, depart, thou art an enemy to my salvation. Shall I entertain thee against my sovereign Lord? How then shall I look Him in the face at His coming? Should I now be ashamed of His ways and servants, how can I expect the blessing?[116] But, indeed, this Shame was a bold villain; I could scarce shake him out of my company; yea, he would be haunting of me, and continually whispering me in the ear, with some one or other of the infirmities that attend religion; but at last I told him it was but in vain to attempt further in this business; for those things that he disdained, in those did I see most glory; and so at last I got past this importunate one. And when I had shaken him off, then I began to sing—

The trials that those men do meet withal,
That are obedient to the heavenly call,
Are manifold, and suited to the flesh,
And come, and come, and come again afresh;
That now, or sometime else, we by them may
Be taken, overcome, and cast away.
O let the pilgrims, let the pilgrims, then,
Be vigilant, and quit themselves like men.

CHRISTIAN. I am glad, my brother, that thou didst withstand this villain so bravely; for of all, as thou sayest, I think he has the wrong name; for he is so bold as to follow us in the streets, and to attempt to put us to shame before all men; that is, to make us ashamed of that which is good; but if he were not himself audacious, he would never attempt to do

116 Mark 8:38

as he does. But let us still resist him; for notwithstanding all his bravadoes, he promoteth the fool, and none else. "The wise shall inherit glory," said Solomon, "but shame shall be the promotion of fools".[117]

FAITHFUL. I think we must cry to Him for help against Shame, who would have us to be valiant for the truth upon the earth.

CHRISTIAN. You say true; but did you meet nobody else in that valley?

FAITHFUL. No, not I, for I had sunshine all the rest of the way through that, and also through the Valley of the Shadow of Death.

CHRISTIAN. It was well for you. I am sure it fared far otherwise with me; I had for a long season, as soon almost as I entered into that valley, a dreadful combat with that foul fiend Apollyon; yea, I thought verily he would have killed me, especially when he got me down and crushed me under him, as if he would have crushed me to pieces; for as he threw me, my sword flew out of my hand; nay, he told me he was sure of me; but I cried to God, and He heard me, and delivered me out of all my troubles. Then I entered into the Valley of the Shadow of Death, and had no light for almost half the way through it. I thought I should have been killed there, over and over; but at last day broke, and the sun rose, and I went through that which was behind with far more ease and quiet.

Moreover, I saw in my dream, that as they went on, Faithful, as he chanced to look on one side, saw a man whose name is Talkative, walking at a distance besides them; for in this place, there was room enough for them all to walk. He was a tall man, and something more comely at a distance

117 Prov. 3:35

than at hand. To this man Faithful addressed himself in this manner.

FAITHFUL. Friend, whither away? Are you going to the heavenly country?

TALKATIVE. I am going to the same place.

FAITHFUL. That is well; then I hope we may have your good company.

TALKATIVE. With a very good will, will I be your companion.

FAITHFUL. Come on, then, and let us go together, and let us spend our time in discoursing of things that are profitable.

TALKATIVE. To talk of things that are good, to me is very acceptable, with you, or with any other; and I am glad that I have met with those that incline to so good a work; for, to speak the truth, there are but few that care thus to spend their time (as they are in their travels), but choose much rather to be speaking of things to no profit; and this hath been a trouble to me.

FAITHFUL. That is indeed a thing to be lamented; for what things so worthy of the use of the tongue and mouth of men on earth, as are the things of the God of Heaven?

TALKATIVE. I like you wonderful well, for your sayings are full of conviction; and I will add, what thing is so pleasant, and what so profitable, as to talk of the things of God? What things so pleasant (that is, if a man hath any delight in things that are wonderful)? For instance, if a man doth delight to talk of the history or the mystery of things; or if a man doth love to talk of miracles, wonders, or signs, where shall he find things recorded so delightful, and so sweetly penned, as in the Holy Scripture?

FAITHFUL. That is true; but to be profited by such things in our talk should be that which we design.

TALKATIVE. That is it that I said; for to talk of such things is most profitable; for by so doing, a man may get knowledge of many things; as of the vanity of earthly things, and the benefit of things above. Thus, in general, but more particularly, by this, a man may learn the necessity of the new birth; the insufficiency of our works; the need of Christ's righteousness, etc. Besides, by this a man may learn, by talk, what it is to repent, to believe, to pray, to suffer, or the like; by this also a man may learn what are the great promises and consolations of the Gospel, to his own comfort. Further, by this a man may learn to refute false opinions, to vindicate the truth, and also to instruct the ignorant.121

FAITHFUL. All this is true, and glad am I to hear these things from you.

TALKATIVE. Alas! the want of this is the cause why so few understand the need of faith, and the necessity of a work of grace in their soul, in order to eternal life; but ignorantly live in the works of the law, by which a man can by no means obtain the kingdom of Heaven.

FAITHFUL. But, by your leave, heavenly knowledge of these is the gift of God; no man attaineth to them by human industry, or only by the talk of them.

TALKATIVE. All this I know very well. For a man can receive nothing, except it be given him from Heaven; all is of grace, not of works. I could give you a hundred scriptures for the confirmation of this.

FAITHFUL. Well, then, said Faithful, what is that one thing that we shall at this time found our discourse upon?

TALKATIVE. What you will. I will talk of things heavenly, or things earthly; things moral, or things evangelical; things sacred, or things profane; things past, or things to come; things foreign, or things at home; things more essential, or things circumstantial; provided that all be done to our profit.

FAITHFUL. Now did Faithful begin to wonder; and stepping to Christian (for he walked all this while by himself), he said to him (but softly), What a brave companion have we got! Surely this man will make a very excellent pilgrim.

CHRISTIAN. At this Christian modestly smiled, and said, This man, with whom you are so taken, will beguile, with that tongue of his, of them that know him not.

FAITHFUL. Do you know him, then?

CHRISTIAN. Know him! Yes, better than he knows himself.

FAITHFUL. Pray, what is he?

CHRISTIAN. His name is Talkative; he dwelleth in our town; I wonder that you should be a stranger to him, only I consider that our town is large.

FAITH. Whose son is he? And whereabout does he dwell?

CHRISTIAN. He is the son of one Say-well; he dwelt in Prating Row; and he is known of all that are acquainted with him, by the name of Talkative in Prating Row; and notwithstanding his fine tongue, he is but a sorry fellow.

FAITHFUL. Well, he seems to be a very pretty man.

CHRISTIAN. That is, to them who have not thorough acquaintance with him; for he is best abroad; near home, he is ugly enough. Your saying that he is a pretty man, brings to my mind what I have observed in the work of the painter, whose pictures show best at a distance, but, very near, more unpleasing.

FAITHFUL. But I am ready to think you do but jest, because you smiled.

CHRISTIAN. God forbid that I should jest (although I smiled) in this matter, or that I should accuse any falsely! I will give you a further discovery of him. This man is for any company, and for any talk; as he talketh now with you, so will he talk when he is on the ale-bench; and the more drink he hath in his crown, the more of these things he hath in his mouth; religion hath no place in his heart, or house, or conversation; all he hath, lieth in his tongue, and his religion is to make a noise therewith.

FAITHFUL. Say you so! then am I in this man greatly deceived.

CHRISTIAN. Deceived! you may be sure of it; remember the proverb, "They say, and do not".[118] But the "kingdom of God is not in word, but in power".[119] He talketh of prayer, of repentance, of faith, and of the new birth; but he knows but only to talk of them. I have been in his family, and have observed him both at home and abroad; and I know what I say of him is the truth. His house is as empty of religion, as the white of an egg is of savour. There is there, neither prayer, nor sign of repentance for sin; yea, the brute in his kind serves God far better than he. He is the very stain, reproach, and shame of religion, to all that know him; it can hardly have a good word in all that end of the town where he dwells, through him.[120] Thus say the common people that know him, A saint abroad, and a devil at home. His poor family finds it so, he is such a churl, such a railer at, and so unreasonable with his servants, that they neither know how to do for, or speak to him. Men that have any dealings with him, say, it is better to deal with a Turk than with him; for fairer dealing they shall have at their hands. This Talkative (if it be possible) will go beyond them, defraud, beguile, and over-reach them. Besides, he brings up his sons to follow his steps; and if he findeth in any of them a foolish timorousness (for so he calls the first appearance of a tender conscience), he calls them fools, and blockheads, and by no means will employ them in much, or speak to their commendations before others. For my part, I am of opinion, that he has, by

118 Matt. 23:3

119 1 Cor. 4:20

120 Rom. 2:24, 25

his wicked life, caused many to stumble and fall; and will be, if God prevent not, the ruin of many more.

FAITHFUL. Well, my brother, I am bound to believe you; not only because you say you know him, but also because, like a Christian, you make your reports of men. For I cannot think that you speak these things of ill-will, but because it is even so as you say.

CHRISTIAN. Had I known him no more than you, I might perhaps have thought of him as, at the first, you did; yea, had he received this report at their hands only that are enemies to religion, I should have thought it had been a slander—a lot that often falls from bad men's mouths upon good men's names and professions; but all these things, yea, and a great many more as bad, of my own knowledge, I can prove him guilty of. Besides, good men are ashamed of him; they can neither call him brother, nor friend; the very naming of him among them makes them blush, if they know him.

FAITHFUL. Well, I see that saying and doing are two things, and hereafter I shall better observe this distinction.

CHRISTIAN. They are two things indeed, and are as diverse as are the soul and the body; for as the body without the soul is but a dead carcass, so saying, if it be alone, is but a dead carcass also. The soul of religion is the practical part: "Pure religion and undefiled, before God and the Father, is this, to visit the fatherless and widows in their affliction, and to keep himself unspotted from the world".[121] This Talkative is not aware of; he thinks that hearing and saying will make a good Christian, and thus he deceiveth his own soul. Hearing is but as the sowing of the seed; talking is not sufficient to prove that fruit is indeed in the heart and life; and let us assure ourselves, that at the day of doom men shall be

121 James 1:27; see vv. 22–26

judged according to their fruits.[122] It will not be said then, Did you believe? but, Were you doers, or talkers only? and accordingly shall they be judged. The end of the world is compared to our harvest; and you know men at harvest regard nothing but fruit. Not that anything can be accepted that is not of faith, but I speak this to show you how insignificant the profession of Talkative will be at that day.

FAITHFUL. This brings to my mind that of Moses, by which he describeth the beast that is clean.[123] He is such a one that parteth the hoof and cheweth the cud; not that parteth the hoof only, or that cheweth the cud only. The hare cheweth the cud, but yet is unclean, because be parteth not the hoof. And this truly resembleth Talkative, he cheweth the cud, he seeketh knowledge, he cheweth upon the word; but he divideth not the hoof, he parteth not with the way of sinners; but, as the hare, he retaineth the foot of a dog or bear, and therefore he is unclean.

CHRISTIAN. You have spoken, for aught I know, the true Gospel sense of those texts. And I will add another thing: Paul calleth some men, yea, and those great talkers too, "sounding brass, and tinkling cymbals," that is, as he expounds them in another place, "things without life, giving sound".[124] Things without life, that is, without the true faith and grace of the Gospel; and consequently, things that shall never be placed in the kingdom of Heaven among those that are the children of life; though their sound, by their talk, be as if it were the tongue or voice of an angel.

FAITHFUL. Well, I was not so fond of his company at first, but I am as sick of it now. What shall we do to be rid of him?

122 Matt. 13:25

123 Lev. 11; Deut. 14

124 1 Cor. 13:1–3; 14:7

CHRISTIAN. Take my advice, and do as I bid you, and you shall find that he will soon be sick of your company too, except God shall touch his heart, and turn it.

FAITHFUL. What would you have me to do?

CHRISTIAN. Why, go to him, and enter into some serious discourse about the power of religion; and ask him plainly (when he has approved of it, for that he will) whether this thing be set up in his heart, house, or conversation?

FAITHFUL. Then Faithful stepped forward again, and said to Talkative, Come, what cheer? How is it now?

TALKATIVE. Thank you, well. I thought we should have had a great deal of talk by this time.

FAITHFUL. Well, if you will, we will fall to it now; and since you left it with me to state the question, let it be this: How doth the saving grace of God discover itself, when it is in the heart of man?

TALKATIVE. I perceive then, that our talk must be about the power of things. Well, it is a very good question, and I shall be willing to answer you. And take my answer in brief, thus: First, Where the grace of work of God is in the heart, it causeth there a great outcry against sin. Secondly—

FAITHFUL. Nay, hold, let us consider of one at once. I think you should rather say, It shows itself by inclining the soul to abhor its sin.

TALKATIVE. Why, what difference is there between crying out against, and abhorring of sin?

FAITHFUL. O! a great deal. A man may cry out against sin of policy, but he cannot abhor it, but by virtue of a godly antipathy against it. I have heard many cry out against sin in the pulpit, who yet can abide it well enough in the heart, house, and conversation. Joseph's mistress cried out with a loud voice, as if she had been very holy; but she would willingly, notwithstanding that, have committed uncleanness with him.[125] Some cry out against sin, even as the mother cries out against her child in her lap, when she calleth it slut and naughty girl, and then falls to hugging and kissing it.

TALKATIVE. You lie at the catch, I perceive.

FAITHFUL. No, not I; I am only for setting things right. But what is the second thing whereby you would prove a discovery of a work of grace in the heart?

TALKATIVE. Great knowledge of Gospel mysteries.

FAITHFUL. This sign should have been first; but first or last, it is also false; for knowledge, great knowledge, may be obtained in the mysteries of the Gospel, and yet no work of grace in the soul.[126] Yea, if a man have all knowledge, he may yet be nothing, and so consequently be no child of God. When Christ said, "Do you know all these things?" and the disciples had answered, Yes; He addeth, "Blessed are ye if ye do them." He doth not lay the blessing in the knowing of them, but in the doing of them. For there is a knowledge that is not attended with doing: "He that knoweth his master's will, and doeth it not." A man may know like an angel, and yet be no Christian, therefore your sign of it is not true. Indeed, to know is a thing that pleaseth talkers and boasters; but to do is that which pleaseth God. Not that the heart can be good without knowledge; for without that the heart is naught. There is, therefore, knowledge and knowledge. Knowledge that resteth in the bare speculation of things; and knowledge that is accompanied with the grace of faith and love; which puts a man upon doing even the will of God from the heart: the first of these will serve the talker; but without the other the true Christian is not content. "Give

125 Gen. 39:15
126 1 Cor. 13

me understanding, and I shall keep Thy law; yea, I shall observe it with my whole heart".[127]

TALKATIVE. You lie at the catch again; this is not for edification.

FAITHFUL. Well, if you please, propound another sign how this work of grace discovereth itself where it is.

TALKATIVE. Not I, for I see we shall not agree.

FAITHFUL. Well, if you will not, will you give me leave to do it?

TALKATIVE. You may use your liberty.

FAITHFUL. A work of grace in the soul discovereth itself, either to him that hath it, or to standers by.

To him that hath it thus: It gives him conviction of sin, especially of the defilement of his nature and the sin of unbelief (for the sake of which he is sure to be damned, if he findeth not mercy at God's hand, by faith in Jesus Christ.[128] This sight and sense of things worketh in him sorrow and shame for sin; he findeth, moreover, revealed in Him the Saviour of the world, and the absolute necessity of closing with Him for life, at the which he findeth hungerings and thirstings after Him; to which hungerings, etc., the promise is made.[129] Now, according to the strength or weakness of his faith in his Saviour, so is his joy and peace, so is his love to holiness, so are his desires to know Him more, and also to serve Him in this world. But though I say it discovereth itself thus unto him, yet it is but seldom that he is able to conclude that this is a work of grace; because his corruptions now, and his abused reason, make his mind to misjudge in this matter; therefore, in him that hath this work, there is

127 Psa. 119:34

128 John 16:8; Rom. 7:24; John 16:9; Mark 16:16

129 Psa. 38:18; Jer. 31:19; Gal. 2:16; Acts 4:12; Matt. 5:6; Rev. 21:26

required a very sound judgment before he can, with steadiness, conclude that this is a work of grace.

To others, it is thus discovered:

1. By an experimental confession of his faith in Christ[130]

2. By a life answerable to that confession; to wit, a life of holiness; heart-holiness, family-holiness (if he hath a family), and by conversation-holiness in the world; which, in the general, teacheth him, inwardly, to abhor his sin, and himself for that, in secret; to suppress it in his family, and to promote holiness in the world; not by talk only, as a hypocrite or talkative person may do, but by a practical subjection, in faith and love, to the power of the Word.[131] And now, Sir, as to this brief description of the work of grace, and also the discovery of it, if you have aught to object, object; if not, then give me leave to propound to you a second question.

TALKATIVE. Nay, my part is not now to object, but to hear; let me, therefore, have your second question.

FAITHFUL. It is this: Do you experience this first part of this description of it? and doth your life and conversation testify the same? or standeth your religion in word or in tongue, and not in deed and truth? Pray, if you incline to answer me in this, say no more than you know the God above will say Amen to; and, also, nothing but what your conscience can justify you in; "for, not he that commendeth himself is approved, but whom the Lord commendeth." Besides, to say, I am thus, and thus, when my conversation, and all my neighbours, tell me I lie, is great wickedness.

TALKATIVE. Then Talkative at first began to blush; but, recovering himself, thus he replied: You come now to experience, to conscience, and God; and to appeal to Him for justification of what is spoken. This kind of discourse I

130 Rom. 10:10; Phil. 1:27; Matt. 5:19

131 John 14:15; Psa. 1:2–3; Job 42:5, 6; Ezek. 20:43

did not expect; nor am I disposed to give an answer to such questions, because I count not myself bound thereto, unless you take upon you to be a catechiser, and, though you should so do, yet I may refuse to make you my judge. But, I pray, will you tell me why you ask me such questions?

FAITHFUL. Because I saw you forward to talk, and because I knew not that you had aught else but notion. Besides, to tell you all the truth, I have heard of you, that you are a man whose religion lies in talk, and that your conversation gives this your mouth-profession the lie. They say, you are a spot among Christians; and that religion fareth the worse for your ungodly conversation; that some already have stumbled at your wicked ways, and that more are in danger of being destroyed thereby; your religion, and an ale-house, and covetousness, and uncleanness, and swearing, and lying, and vain company keeping, etc., will stand together. The proverb is true of you which is said of a whore, to wit, that she is a shame to all women; so are you a shame to all professors.

TALKATIVE. Since you are ready to take up reports, and to judge so rashly as you do, I cannot but conclude you are some peevish or melancholy man, not fit to be discoursed with; and so adieu.

CHRISTIAN. Then came up Christian, and said to his brother, I told you how it would happen; your words and his lusts could not agree; he had rather leave your company than reform his life. But he is gone, as I said; let him go, the loss is no man's but his own; he has saved us the trouble of going from him; for he continuing (as I suppose he will do) as he is, he would have been but a blot in our company; besides, the apostle says, "From such withdraw thyself."

FAITHFUL. But I am glad we had this little discourse with him; it may happen that he will think of it again; however, I have dealt plainly with him, and so am clear of his blood, if he perisheth.

CHRISTIAN. You did well to talk so plainly to him as you did; there is but little of this faithful dealing with men now-a-days, and that makes religion to stink so in the nostrils of many, as it doth; for they are these talkative fools whose religion is only in word, and are debauched and vain in their conversation, that (being so much admitted into the fellowship of the godly) do puzzle the world, blemish Christianity, and grieve the sincere. I wish that all men would deal with such as you have done; then should they either be made more conformable to religion, or the company of saints would be too hot for them. Then did Faithful say,

How Talkative at first lifts up his plumes!
How bravely doth he speak! How he presumes
To drive down all before him! But so soon
As Faithful talks of heart-work, like the moon
That's past the full, into the wane he goes.
And so will all, but he that HEART-WORK knows.

Thus they went on talking of what they had seen by the way, and so made that way easy which would, otherwise, no doubt, have been tedious to them; for now they went through a wilderness.

Now, when they were got almost quite out of this wilderness, Faithful chanced to cast his eye back, and espied one coming after them, and he knew him. Oh! said Faithful to his brother, Who comes yonder? Then Christian looked, and said, It is my good friend Evangelist. Aye, and my good friend too, said Faithful, for it was he that set me the way to the gate. Now was Evangelist come up unto them, and thus saluted them:

EVANGELIST. Peace be with you, dearly beloved; and peace be to your helpers.

CHRISTIAN. Welcome, welcome, my good Evangelist; the sight of thy countenance brings to my remembrance thy ancient kindness and unwearied labouring for my eternal good.

FAITHFUL. And a thousand times welcome, said good Faithful. Thy company, O sweet Evangelist, how desirable it is to us poor pilgrims!

EVANGELIST. Then said Evangelist, How hath it fared with you, my friends, since the time of our last parting? What have you met with, and how have you behaved yourselves?

Then Christian and Faithful told him of all things that had happened to them in the way; and how and with what difficulty, they had arrived to that place.

EVANGELIST. Right glad am I, said Evangelist, not that you have met with trials, but that you have been victors; and for that you have, notwithstanding many weaknesses, continued in the way to this very day.

I say, right glad am I of this thing, and that for mine own sake and yours. I have sowed, and you have reaped; and the day is coming, when both he that sowed and they that reaped shall rejoice together; that is, if you hold out; "for in due season ye shall reap, if ye faint not".[132] The crown is before you, and it is an incorruptible one; "so run, that you may obtain" it.[133] Some there be that set out for this crown, and, after they have gone far for it, another comes in, and takes it from them; hold fast, therefore, that you have, let no man take your crown.[134] You are not yet out of

132 John 4:36; Gal. 6:9

133 1 Cor. 9:24–27

134 Rev. 3:11

the gun-shot of the devil; you have not resisted unto blood, striving against sin; let the kingdom be always before you, and believe steadfastly concerning things that are invisible. Let nothing that is on this side the other world get within you; and, above all, look well to your own hearts, and to the lusts thereof, "for they are deceitful above all things, and desperately wicked"; set your faces like a flint; you have all power in Heaven and earth on your side.

CHRISTIAN. Then Christian thanked him for his exhortation; but told him, withal, that they would have him speak further to them for their help the rest of the way, and the rather, for that they well knew that he was a prophet, and could tell them of things that might happen unto them, and also how they might resist and overcome them. To which request Faithful also consented. So Evangelist began as followeth:

EVANGELIST. My sons, you have heard in the words of the truth of the Gospel that you must, through many tribulations, enter into the kingdom of Heaven. And again, that in every city bonds and afflictions abide in you; and therefore you cannot expect that you should go long on your pilgrimage without them, in some sort or other. You have found something of the truth of these testimonies upon you already, and more will immediately follow; for now, as you see, you are almost out of this wilderness, and therefore you will soon come into a town that you will by and by see before you; and in that town you will be hardly beset with enemies, who will strain hard but they will kill you; and be you sure that one or both of you must seal the testimony which you hold, with blood; but be you faithful unto death, and the King will give you a crown of life. He that shall die there, although his death will be unnatural, and his pain perhaps great, he will yet have the better of his fellow; not only because he will be arrived at the Celestial City soonest, but because he will escape many miseries that the other will meet with in the rest of his journey. But when you are come to the town, and shall find fulfilled what I have here related, then remember your friend and quit yourselves like men, and commit the keeping of your souls to your God in well-doing, as unto a faithful Creator.

Then I saw in my dream, that when they were got out of the wilderness, they presently saw a town before them, and the name of that town is Vanity; and at the town there is a fair kept, called Vanity Fair: it is kept all the year long; it beareth the name of Vanity Fair, because the town where it is kept is lighter than vanity; and also because all that is there sold, or that cometh thither, is vanity. As is the saying of the wise, "All that cometh is vanity".[135]

This fair is no new-erected business, but a thing of ancient standing; I will show you the original of it.

Almost 5,000 years agone, there were pilgrims walking to the Celestial City as these two honest persons are: and Beelzebub, Apollyon, and Legion, with their companions, perceiving by the path that the pilgrims made, that their way to the city lay through this town of Vanity, they contrived here to set up a fair; a fair wherein should be sold all sorts of vanity, and that it should last all the year long: therefore at this fair are all such merchandise sold, as houses, lands, trades, places, honours, preferments, titles, countries, kingdoms, lusts, pleasures, and delights of all sorts, as whores, bawds, wives, husbands, children, masters, servants, lives, blood, bodies, souls, silver, gold, pearls, precious stones, and what not. And, moreover, at this fair there is at all times, to be seen juggling, cheats, games, plays, fools, apes, knaves, and rogues, and that of every kind.

Here are to be seen too, and that for nothing, thefts,

135 Eccl. 1; 2:11, 17; 11:8; Isa. 40:17

murders, adulteries, false swearers, and that of a blood-red colour.

And as in other fairs of less moment, there are the several rows and streets, under their proper names, where such and such wares are vended; so here likewise you have the proper places, rows, streets (viz. countries and kingdoms), where the wares of this fair are soonest to be found. Here is the Britain Row, the French Row, the Italian Row, the Spanish Row, the German Row, where several sorts of vanities are to be sold. But, as in other fairs, some one commodity is as the chief of all the fair, so the ware of Rome and her merchandise is greatly promoted in this fair; only our English nation, with some others, have taken a dislike thereat.

Now, as I said, the way to the Celestial City lies just through this town where this lusty fair is kept; and he that will go to the City, and yet not go through this town, must needs "go out of the world".[136] The Prince of princes Himself, when here, went through this town to His own country, and that upon a fair day too; yea, and as I think, it was Beelzebub, the chief lord of this fair, that invited Him to buy of his vanities; yea, would have made Him lord of the fair, would He but have done him reverence as He went through the town.[137] Yea, because He was such a person of honour, Beelzebub had Him from street to street, and showed Him all the kingdoms of the world in a little time, that he might, if possible, allure the Blessed One to cheapen and buy some of his vanities; but He had no mind to the merchandise, and therefore left the town, without laying out so much as one farthing upon these vanities. This fair, therefore, is an ancient thing, of long standing, and a very great fair. Now these Pilgrims, as I said, must needs go through this fair.

136 1 Cor. 5:10

137 Matt. 4:8; Luke 4:5–7

Well, so they did; but, behold, even as they entered into the fair, all the people in the fair were moved, and the town itself as it were in a hubbub about them; and that for several reasons; for—

First, The pilgrims were clothed with such kind of raiment as was diverse from the raiment of any that traded in that fair. The people, therefore, of the fair, made a great gazing upon them: some said they were fools, some they were bedlams, and some they are outlandish men.[138]

Secondly, And as they wondered at their apparel, so they did likewise at their speech; for few could understand what they said; they naturally spoke the language of Canaan, but they that kept the fair were the men of this world; so that, from one end of the fair to the other, they seemed barbarians each to the other.

Thirdly, But that which did not a little amuse the merchandisers was, that these pilgrims set very light by all their wares; they cared not so much as to look upon them; and if they called upon them to buy, they would put their fingers in their ears, and cry, "Turn away mine eyes from beholding vanity," and look upwards, signifying that their trade and traffic was in heaven.[139]

One chanced mockingly, beholding the carriage of the men, to say unto them, What will ye buy? But they, looking gravely upon him, answered, "We buy the truth".[140] At that there was an occasion taken to despise the men the more: some mocking, some taunting, some speaking reproachfully, and some calling upon others to smite them. At last things came to a hubbub, and great stir in the fair, insomuch that all order was confounded. Now was word presently brought

138 1 Cor. 2:7, 8

139 Psa. 119:37; Phil. 3:19, 20

140 Psa. 23:2–3

to the great one of the fair, who quickly came down, and deputed some of his most trusty friends to take these men into examination, about whom the fair was almost overturned. So the men were brought to examination; and they that sat upon them, asked them whence they came, whither they went, and what they did there in such an unusual garb? The men told them, that they were pilgrims and strangers in the world, and that they were going to their own country, which was the heavenly Jerusalem;[141] and that they had given no occasion to the men of the town, nor yet to the merchandisers, thus to abuse them, and to let them in their journey, except it was, for that, when one asked them what they would buy, they said they would buy the truth. But they that were appointed to examine them did not believe them to be any other than bedlams and mad, or else such as came to put all things into a confusion in the fair. Therefore they took them and beat them, and besmeared them with dirt, and then put them into the cage, that they might be made a spectacle to all the men of the fair. There, therefore, they lay for some time, and were made the objects of any man's sport, or malice, or revenge, the great one of the fair laughing still at all that befell them. But the men being patient, and not rendering railing for railing, but contrariwise, blessing, and giving good words for bad, and kindness for injuries done, some men in the fair that were more observing, and less prejudiced than the rest, began to check and blame the baser sort for their continual abuses done by them to the men; they, therefore, in angry manner, let fly at them again, counting them as bad as the men in the cage, and telling them that they seemed confederates, and should be made partakers of their misfortunes. The other replied, that for aught they could see, the men were quiet, and sober, and intended no-

141 Heb. 9:13–16

body any harm; and that there were many that traded in their fair, that were more worthy to be put into the cage, yea, and pillory too, than were the men that they had abused. Thus, after divers words had passed on both sides, the men behaving themselves all the while very wisely and soberly before them, they fell to some blows among themselves, and did harm one to another. Then were these two poor men brought before their examiners again, and there charged as being guilty of the late hubbub that had been in the fair. So they beat them pitifully, and hanged irons upon them, and led them in chains up and down the fair, for an example and a terror to others, lest any should speak in their behalf, or join themselves unto them. But Christian and Faithful behaved themselves yet more wisely, and received the ignominy and shame that was cast upon them, with so much meekness and patience, that it won to their side, though but few in comparison of the rest, several of the men in the fair. This put the other party yet into greater rage, insomuch that they concluded the death of these two men. Wherefore they threatened, that the cage nor irons should serve their turn, but that they should die, for the abuse they had done, and for deluding the men of the fair.

Then were they remanded to the cage again, until further order should be taken with them. So they put them in, and made their feet fast in the stocks.

Here, therefore, they called again to mind what they had heard from their faithful friend Evangelist, and were the more confirmed in their way and sufferings, by what he told them would happen to them. They also now comforted each other, that whose lot it was to suffer, even he should have the best of it; therefore each man secretly wished that he might have that preferment: but committing themselves to the all-wise disposal of Him that ruleth all things, with much content they abode in the condition in which they were, until they should be otherwise disposed of.

Then a convenient time being appointed, they brought them forth to their trial, in order to their condemnation. When the time was come, they were brought before their enemies and arraigned. The Judge's name was Lord Hategood. Their indictment was one and the same in substance, though somewhat varying in form, the contents whereof were this—

"That they were enemies to, and disturbers of their trade; that they had made commotions and divisions in the town, and had won a party to their own most dangerous opinions, in contempt of the law of their prince."

Then Faithful began to answer, that he had only set himself against that which had set itself against Him that is higher than the highest. And, said he, as for disturbance, I make none, being myself a man of peace; the parties that were won to us, were won by beholding our truth and innocence, and they are only turned from the worse to the better. And as to the king you talk of, since be is Beelzebub, the enemy of our Lord, I defy him and all his angels.

Then proclamation was made, that they that had aught to say for their lord the king against the prisoner at the bar, should forthwith appear and give in their evidence. So there came in three witnesses, to wit, Envy, Superstition, and Pickthank. They were then asked if they knew the prisoner at the bar; and what they had to say for their lord the king against him.

Then stood forth Envy, and said to this effect, My Lord, I have known this man a long time, and will attest upon my oath before this honourable bench, that he is—

JUDGE. Hold. Give him his oath. (So they sware him). Then he said—

ENVY. My Lord, this man, notwithstanding his plausible

name, is one of the vilest men in our country. He neither regardeth prince nor people, law nor custom; but doth all that he can to possess all men with certain of his disloyal notions, which he in the general calls principles of faith and holiness. And, in particular, I heard him once myself affirm, that Christianity and the customs of our town of Vanity, were diametrically opposite, and could not be reconciled. By which saying, my Lord, he doth at once not only condemn all our laudable doings, but us in the doing of them.

JUDGE. Then did the Judge say to him, Hast thou any more to say?

ENVY. My Lord, I could say much more, only I would not be tedious to the court. Yet, if need be, when the other gentlemen have given in their evidence, rather than anything shall be wanting that will despatch him, I will enlarge my testimony against him. So he was bid stand by.

Then they called Superstition, and bid him look upon the prisoner. They also asked, what he could say for their lord the king against him. Then they sware him; so he began.

SUPER. My Lord, I have no great acquaintance with this man, nor do I desire to have further knowledge of him; however, this I know, that he is a very pestilent fellow, from some discourse that, the other day, I had with him in this town; for then talking with him, I heard him say, that our religion was naught, and such by which a man could by no means please God. Which sayings of his, my Lord, your Lordship very well knows, what necessarily thence will follow, to wit, that we do still worship in vain, are yet in our sins, and finally shall be damned; and this is that which I have to say.

Then was Pickthank sworn, and bid say what he knew, in behalf of their lord the king, against the prisoner at the bar.

PICKTHANK. My Lord, and you gentlemen all, This fellow I have known of a long time, and have heard him speak things that ought not to be spoke; for he hath railed on our noble prince Beelzebub, and hath spoken contemptibly of his honourable friends, whose names are the Lord Old Man, the Lord Carnal Delight, the Lord Luxurious, the Lord Desire of Vain Glory, my old Lord Lechery, Sir Having Greedy, with all the rest of our nobility; and he hath said, moreover, That if all men were of his mind, if possible, there is not one of these noblemen should have any longer a being in this town. Besides, he hath not been afraid to rail on you, my Lord, who are now appointed to be his judge, calling you an ungodly villain, with many other such like vilifying terms, with which he hath bespattered most of the gentry of our town.

When this Pickthank had told his tale, the Judge directed his speech to the prisoner at the bar, saying, Thou runagate, heretic, and traitor, hast thou heard what these honest gentlemen have witnessed against thee?

FAITHFUL. May I speak a few words in my own defence?

JUDGE. Sirrah! Sirrah! thou deservest to live no longer, but to be slain immediately upon the place; yet, that all men may see our gentleness towards thee, let us hear what thou, vile runagate, hast to say.

FAITHFUL. 1. I say, then, in answer to what Mr. Envy hath spoken, I never said aught but this, That what rule, or laws, or custom, or people, were flat against the Word of God, are diametrically opposite to Christianity. If I have said amiss in this, convince me of my error, and I am ready here before you to make my recantation.

2. As to the second, to wit, Mr. Superstition, and his charge against me, I said only this, That in the worship of God there is required a Divine faith; but there can be no Divine faith without a Divine revelation of the will of God. Therefore, whatever is thrust into the worship of God that is not agreeable to Divine revelation, cannot be done but by

a human faith, which faith will not be profitable to eternal life.

3. As to what Mr. Pickthank hath said, I say (avoiding terms, as that I am said to rail, and the like), that the prince of this town, with all the rabblement, his attendants, by this gentleman named, are more fit for a being in hell, than in this town and country: and so, the Lord have mercy upon me!

Then the Judge called to the jury (who all this while stood by, to hear and observe; Gentlemen of the jury, you see this man about whom so great an uproar hath been made in this town. You have also heard what these worthy gentlemen have witnessed against him. Also you have heard his reply and confession. It lieth now in your breasts to hang him, or save his life; but yet I think meet to instruct you into our law.

There was an Act made in the days of Pharaoh the Great, servant to our prince, that lest those of a contrary religion should multiply, and grow too strong for him, their males should be thrown into the river.[142] There was also an Act made in the days of Nebuchadnezzar the Great, another of his servants, that whosoever would not fall down and worship his golden image, should be thrown into a fiery furnace.[143] There was also an Act made in the days of Darius, that whoso, for some time, called upon any God but him, should be cast into the lions' den.[144] Now the substance of these laws this rebel has broken, not only in thought (which is not to be borne) but also in word and deed; which must therefore needs be intolerable.

For that of Pharaoh, his law was made upon a supposi-

142 Exo. 1

143 Dan. 3

144 Dan. 6

tion, to prevent mischief, no crime being yet apparent; but here is a crime apparent. For the second and third, you see he disputeth against our religion; and for the treason he hath confessed, he deserveth to die the death.

Then went the jury out, whose names were, Mr. Blind-man, Mr. No-good, Mr. Malice, Mr. Love-lust, Mr. Live-loose, Mr. Heady, Mr. High-mind, Mr. Enmity, Mr. Liar, Mr. Cruelty, Mr. Hate-light, and Mr. Implacable; who every one gave in his private verdict against him among themselves, and afterwards unanimously concluded to bring him in guilty before the Judge. And first, among themselves, Mr. Blind-man, the foreman, said, I see clearly that this man is a heretic. Then said Mr. No-good, Away with such a fellow from the earth. Ay, said Mr. Malice, for I hate the very looks of him. Then said Mr. Love-lust, I could never endure him. Nor I, said Mr. Live-loose, for he would always be condemning my way. Hang him, hang him, said Mr. Heady. A sorry scrub, said Mr. High-mind. My heart riseth against him, said Mr. Enmity. He is a rogue, said Mr. Liar. Hanging is too good for him, said Mr. Cruelty. Let us despatch him out of the way, said Mr. Hate-light. Then said Mr. Implacable, Might I have all the world given me, I could not be reconciled to him; therefore, let us forthwith bring him in guilty of death. And so they did; therefore he was presently condemned, to be had from the place where he was, to the place from whence he came, and there to be put to the most cruel death that could be invented.

They, therefore, brought him out, to do with him according to their law; and, first, they scourged him, then they buffeted him, then they lanced his flesh with knives; after that, they stoned him with stones, then pricked him with their swords; and, last of all, they burned him to ashes at the stake. Thus came Faithful to his end.

Now I saw that there stood behind the multitude, a

chariot and a couple of horses, waiting for Faithful, who (so soon as his adversaries had despatched him) was taken up into it, and straightway was carried up through the clouds, with sound of trumpet, the nearest way to the Celestial Gate. But as for Christian, he had some respite, and was remanded back to prison. So he there remained for a space; but He that overrules all things, having the power of their rage in His own hand, so wrought it about, that Christian for that time escaped them, and went his way; and as he went, he sang, saying—

> *Well, Faithful, thou hast faithfully profest Unto thy Lord; with whom thou shalt be blest, When faithless ones, with all their vain delights, Are crying out under their hellish plights, Sing, Faithful, sing, and let thy name survive; For, though they kill'd thee, thou art yet alive.*

CHRISTIAN HAS ANOTHER COMPANION

Now I saw in my dream, that Christian went not forth alone, for there was one whose name was Hopeful (being made so by the beholding of Christian and Faithful in their words and behaviour, in their sufferings at the Fair), who joined himself unto him, and, entering into a brotherly covenant, told him that he would be his companion. Thus, one died to bear testimony to the truth, and another rises out of his ashes, to be a companion with Christian in his pilgrimage. This Hopeful also told Christian, that there were many more of the men in the Fair, that would take their time and follow after.

So I saw that quickly after they were got out of the Fair, they overtook one that was going before them, whose name was By-ends; so they said to him, What countryman, Sir? and how far go you this way? He told them, that he came from the town of Fair-speech, and he was going to the Celestial City, but told them not his name.

From Fair-speech! said Christian. Is there any good that lives there?.[145]

BY-ENDS. Yes, said By-ends, I hope.

CHRISTIAN. Pray, Sir, What may I call you? Said Christian.

145 Prov. 26:25

BY-ENDS. I am a stranger to you, and you to me: if you be going this way, I shall be glad of your company; if not, I must be content.

CHRISTIAN. This town of Fair-speech, said Christian, I have heard of; and, as I remember, they say it is a wealthy place.

BY-ENDS. Yes, I will assure you that it is; and I have very many rich kindred there.

CHRISTIAN. Pray, who are your kindred there? if a man may be so bold.

BY-ENDS. Almost the whole town; and in particular, my Lord Turn-about, my Lord Time-server, my Lord Fair-speech (from whose ancestors that town first took its name), also Mr. Smooth-man, Mr. Facing-both-ways, Mr. Any-thing; and the parson of our parish, Mr. Two-tongues, was my mother's own brother, by father's side; and to tell you the truth, I am become a gentleman of good quality, yet my great-grandfather was but a waterman, looking one way and rowing another, and I got most of my estate by the same occupation.

CHRISTIAN. Are you a married man?

BY-ENDS. Yes, and my wife is a very virtuous woman, the daughter of a virtuous woman; she was my Lady Feigning's daughter, therefore she came of a very honourable family, and is arrived to such a pitch of breeding, that she knows how to carry it to all, even to prince and peasant. It is true we somewhat differ in religion from those of the stricter sort, yet but in two small points; first, we never strive against wind and tide; secondly, we are always most zealous when religion goes in his silver slippers; we love much to walk with him in the street, if the sun shines, and the people applaud him.

Then Christian stepped a little aside to his fellow Hopeful, saying, It runs in my mind that this is one By-ends of

Fair-speech; and if it be he, we have as very a knave in our company, as dwelleth in all these parts. Then said Hopeful, Ask him; methinks he should not be ashamed of his name. So Christian came up with him again, and said, Sir, you talk as if you knew something more than all the world doth; and if I take not my mark amiss, I deem I have half a guess of you: Is not your name Mr. By-ends, of Fair-speech?

BY-ENDS. This is not my name, but indeed it is a nickname that is given me by some that cannot abide me; and I must be content to bear it as a reproach, as other good men have borne theirs before me.

CHRISTIAN. But did you never give an occasion to men to call you by this name?

BY-ENDS. Never, never! The worst that ever I did to give them an occasion to give me this name was, that I had always the luck to jump in my judgment with the present way of the times, whatever it was, and my chance was to get thereby; but if things are thus cast upon me, let me count them a blessing; but let not the malicious load me therefore with reproach.

CHRISTIAN. I thought, indeed, that you were the man that I heard of; and to tell you what I think, I fear this name belongs to you more properly than you are willing we should think it doth.

BY-ENDS. Well, if you will thus imagine, I cannot help it; you shall find me a fair company-keeper, if you will still admit me your associate.

CHRISTIAN. If you will go with us, you must go against wind and tide; the which, I perceive, is against your opinion; you must also own religion in his rags, as well as when in his silver slippers; and stand by him, too, when bound in irons, as well as when he walketh the streets with applause.

BY-ENDS. You must not impose, nor lord it over my faith; leave me to my liberty, and let me go with you.

CHRISTIAN. Not a step further, unless you will do in what I propound, as we.

Then said By-ends, I shall never desert my old principles, since they are harmless and profitable. If I may not go with you, I must do as I did before you overtook me, even go by myself, until some overtake me that will be glad of my company.

Now I saw in my dream, that Christian and Hopeful forsook him, and kept their distance before him; but one of them looking back, saw three men following Mr. By-ends, and behold, as they came up with him, he made them a very low conge; and they also gave him a compliment. The men's names were Mr. Hold-the-world, Mr. Money-love, and Mr. Save-all; men that Mr. By-ends had formerly been acquainted with; for in their minority they were schoolfellows, and were taught by one Mr. Gripeman, a schoolmaster in Love-gain, which is a market town in the county of Coveting, in the north. This schoolmaster taught them the art of getting, either by violence, cozenage, flattery, lying, or by putting on a guise of religion; and these four gentlemen had attained much of the art of their master, so that they could each of them have kept such a school themselves.

Well, when they had, as I said, thus saluted each other, Mr. Money-love said to Mr. By-ends, Who are they upon the road before us? (for Christian and Hopeful were yet within view).

BY-ENDS. They are a couple of far countrymen, that, after their mode, are going on pilgrimage.

MONEY-LOVE. Alas! Why did they not stay, that we might have had their good company? for they, and we, and you, Sir, I hope, are all going on a pilgrimage.

BY-ENDS. We are so, indeed; but the men before us are so rigid, and love so much their own notions, and do also so lightly esteem the opinions of others, that let a man be never so godly, yet if he jumps not with them in all things, they thrust him quite out of their company.

SAVE-ALL. That is bad, but we read of some that are righteous overmuch; and such men's rigidness prevails with them to judge and condemn all but themselves. But, I pray, what, and how many, were the things wherein you differed?

BY-ENDS. Why, they, after their headstrong manner, conclude that it is duty to rush on their journey all weathers; and I am for waiting for wind and tide. They are for hazarding all for God at a clap; and I am for taking all advantages to secure my life and estate. They are for holding their notions, though all other men are against them; but I am for religion in what, and so far as the times, and my safety, will bear it. They are for religion when in rags and contempt; but I am for him when he walks in his golden slippers, in the sunshine, and with applause.

MR. HOLD-THE-WORLD. Aye, and hold you there still, good Mr. By-ends; for, for my part, I can count him but a fool, that, having the liberty to keep what he has, shall be so unwise as to lose it. Let us be wise as serpents; it is best to make hay when the sun shines; you see how the bee lieth still all winter, and bestirs her only when she can have profit with pleasure. God sends sometimes rain, and sometimes sunshine; if they be such fools to go through the first, yet let us be content to take fair weather along with us. For my part, I like that religion best, that will stand with the security of God's good blessings unto us; for who can imagine, that is ruled by his reason, since God has bestowed upon us the good things of this life, but that He would have us keep them for His sake? Abraham and Solomon grew rich in religion. And Job says, that a good man shall lay up gold as dust. But he must not be such as the men before us, if they be as you have described them.

MR. SAVE-ALL. I think that we are all agreed in this matter, and therefore there needs no more words about it.

MR. MONEY-LOVE. No, there needs no more words about this matter indeed; for he that believes neither Scripture nor reason (and you see we have both on our side), neither knows his own liberty, nor seeks his own safety.

MR. BY-ENDS. My brethren, we are, as you see, going all on pilgrimage; and for our better diversion from things that are bad, give me leave to propound unto you this question: Suppose a man, a minister, or a tradesman, etc., should have an advantage lie before him, to get the good blessings of this life, yet so as that he can by no means come by them except, in appearance at least, he becomes extraordinary zealous in some points of religion that he meddled not with before; may he not use this means to attain his end, and yet be a right honest man?

MR. MONEY-LOVE. I see the bottom of your question; and, with these gentlemen's good leave, I will endeavour to shape you an answer. And first to speak to your question as it concerns a minister himself: Suppose a minister, a worthy man, possessed but of a very small benefice, and has in his eye a greater, more fat, and plump by far; he has also now an opportunity of getting of it, yet so as by being more studious, by preaching more frequently, and zealously, and, because the temper of the people requires it, by altering of some of his principles; for my part, I see no reason but a man may do this (provided he has a call), aye, and more a great deal besides, and yet be an honest man. For why—

1. His desire of a greater benefice is lawful (this cannot be contradicted), since it is set before him by Providence; so then, he may get it, if he can, making no question for conscience sake.

2. Besides, his desire after that benefice makes him more studious, a more zealous preacher, etc., and so makes him a

better man; yea, makes him better improve his parts, which is according to the mind of God.

3. Now, as for his complying with the temper of his people, by dissenting, to serve them, some of his principles, this argueth—(1). That he is of a self-denying temper. (2). Of a sweet and winning deportment. And so (3). More fit for the ministerial function.

4. I conclude then, that a minister that changes a small for a great, should not, for so doing, be judged as covetous; but rather, since he is improved in his parts and industry thereby, be counted as one that pursues his call, and the opportunity put into his hand to do good.

And now to the second part of the question, which concerns the tradesman you mentioned. Suppose such an one to have but a poor employ in the world, but by becoming religious, he may mend his market, perhaps get a rich wife, or more, and far better customers to his shop; for my part, I see no reason but that this may be lawfully done. For why—

1. To become religious is a virtue, by what means soever a man becomes so.

2. Nor is it unlawful to get a rich wife, or more custom to my shop.

3. Besides, the man that gets these by becoming religious, gets that which is good, of them that are good, by becoming good himself; so then here is a good wife, and good customers, and good gain, and all these by becoming religious, which is good; therefore, to become religious to get all these, is a good and profitable design.

This answer, thus made by this Mr. Money-love to Mr. By-end's question, was highly applauded by them all; wherefore they concluded, upon the whole, that it was most wholesome and advantageous. And because, as they thought, no man was able to contradict it, and because Christian and Hopeful were yet within call, they jointly agreed to assault them with the question as soon as they overtook them; and the rather because they had opposed Mr. By-ends before. So they called after them, and they stopped, and stood still till they came up to them; but they concluded, as they went, that not Mr. By-ends, but old Mr. Hold-the-world, should propound the question to them, because, as they supposed, their answer to him would be without the remainder of that heat that was kindled betwixt Mr. By-ends and them, at their parting a little before.

So they came up to each other, and after a short salutation, Mr. Hold-the-world propounded the question to Christian and his fellow, and bid them to answer it if they could.

CHRISTIAN. Then said Christian, Even a babe in religion may answer 10,000 such questions. For if it be unlawful to follow Christ for loaves (as it is in the sixth of John), how much more abominable is it to make of him and religion a stalking-horse, to get and enjoy the world! Nor do we find any other than heathens, hypocrites, devils, and witches, that are of this opinion.

1. Heathens; for when Hamor and Shechem had a mind to the daughter and cattle of Jacob, and saw that there was no ways for them to come at them, but by becoming circumcised; they say to their companions, if every male of us be circumcised, as they are circumcised, shall not their cattle, and their substance, and every beast of theirs, be ours? Their daughter and their cattle were that which they sought to obtain, and their religion the stalking-horse they made use of to come at them. Read the whole story.[146]

2. The hypocritical Pharisees were also of this religion; long prayers were their pretence; but to get widows' houses

146 Gen. 34:20–23

was their intent; and greater damnation was from God their judgment (Luke 20:46, 47).

3. Judas the devil was also of this religion; he was religious for the bag, that he might be possessed of what was therein; but he was lost, cast away, and the very son of perdition.

4. Simon the witch was of this religion too; for he would have had the Holy Ghost, that he might have got money therewith; and his sentence from Peter's mouth was according.[147]

5. Neither will it out of my mind, but that that man that takes up religion for the world, will throw away religion for the world; for so surely as Judas designed the world in becoming religious, so surely did he also sell religion and his Master for the same. To answer the question therefore affirmatively, as I perceive you have done; and to accept of, as authentic, such answer, is both heathenish, hypocritical, and devilish; and your reward will be according to your works. Then they stood staring one upon another, but had not wherewith to answer Christian. Hopeful also approved of the soundness of Christian's answer; so there was a great silence among them. Mr. By-ends and his company also staggered and kept behind, that Christian and Hopeful might outgo them. Then said Christian to his fellow, If these men cannot stand before the sentence of men, what will they do with the sentence of God? And if they are mute when dealt with by vessels of clay, what will they do when they shall be rebuked by the flames of a devouring fire?

Then Christian and Hopeful outwent them again, and went till they came at a delicate plain, called Ease, where they went with much content; but that plain was but narrow, so they were quickly got over it. Now at the further side

147 Acts 8:19–20

of that plain, was a little Hill called Lucre, and in that hill a silver mine, which some of them that had formerly gone that way, because of the rarity of it, had turned aside to see; but going too near the brink of the pit, the ground being deceitful under them, broke, and they were slain; some also had been maimed there, and could not, to their dying day, be their own men again.

Then I saw in my dream, that a little off the road, over against the silver mine, stood Demas (gentleman-like) to call to passengers to come and see; who said to Christian and his fellow, Ho! turn aside hither, and I will show you a thing.

CHRISTIAN. What thing so deserving as to turn us out of the way to see it?

DEMAS. Here is a silver mine, and some digging in it for treasure. If you will come, with a little pains you may richly provide for yourselves.

HOPEFUL. Then said Hopeful, Let us go see.

CHRISTIAN. Not I, said Christian, I have heard of this place before now; and how many have there been slain; and besides that, treasure is a snare to those that seek it; for it hindereth them in their pilgrimage. Then Christian called to Demas, saying, Is not the place dangerous? Hath it not hindered many in their pilgrimage?[148]

DEMAS. Not very dangerous, except to those that are careless (but withal, he blushed as he spake).

CHRISTIAN. Then said Christian to Hopeful, Let us not stir a step, but still keep on our way.

HOPEFUL. I will warrant you, when By-ends comes up, if he hath the same invitation as we, he will turn in thither to see.

CHRISTIAN. No doubt thereof, for his principles lead him that way, and a hundred to one but he dies there.

148 Hosea 14:8

DEMAS. Then Demas called again, saying, But will you not come over and see?

CHRISTIAN. Then Christian roundly answered, saying, Demas, thou art an enemy to the right ways of the Lord of this way, and hast been already condemned for thine own turning aside, by one of his Majesty's judges;[149] and why seekest thou to bring us into the like condemnation? Besides, if we at all turn aside, our Lord the King will certainly hear thereof, and will there put us to shame, where we would stand with boldness before Him. Demas cried again, That he also was one of their fraternity; and that if they would tarry a little, he also himself would walk with them.

CHRISTIAN. Then said Christian, What is thy name? Is it not the same by the which I have called thee?

DEMAS. Yes, my name is Demas; I am the son of Abraham.

CHRISTIAN. I know you; Gehazi was your great-grandfather, and Judas your father; and you have trod in their steps.[150] It is but a devilish prank that thou usest; thy father was hanged for a traitor, and thou deservest no better reward. Assure thyself, that when we come to the King, we will do Him word of this thy behaviour. Thus they went their way.

By this time By-ends and his companions were come again within sight, and they, at the first beck, went over to Demas. Now, whether they fell into the pit by looking over the brink thereof, or whether they went down to dig, or whether they were smothered in the bottom by the damps that commonly arise, of these things I am not certain; but this I observed, that they never were seen again in the way. Then sang Christian—

149 2 Tim. 4:10

150 2 Kings 5:20; Matt. 26:14, 15; 27:1–5

By-ends and silver Demas both agree;
One calls, the other runs, that he may be
A sharer in his lucre; so these do
Take up in this world, and no further go.

Now I saw that, just on the other side of this plain, the Pilgrims came to a place where stood an old monument, hard by the highway side; at the sight of which they were both concerned, because of the strangeness of the form thereof; for it seemed to them as if it had been a woman transformed into the shape of a pillar; here therefore they stood looking, and looking upon it, but could not for a time tell what they should make thereof. At last Hopeful espied written above the head thereof, a writing in an unusual hand; but he being no scholar, called to Christian (for he was learned) to see if he could pick out the meaning; so he came, and after a little laying of letters together, he found the same to be this, "Remember Lot's wife." So he read it to his fellow; after which they both concluded that that was the pillar of salt into which Lot's wife was turned, for her looking back with a covetous heart, when she was going from Sodom for safety;[151] which sudden and amazing sight gave them occasion of this discourse.

CHRISTIAN. Ah, my brother! this is a seasonable sight; it came opportunely to us after the invitation which Demas gave us to come over to view the Hill Lucre; and had we gone over, as he desired us, and as thou wast inclining to do, my brother, we had, for aught I know, been made ourselves like this woman, a spectacle for those that shall come after to behold.

HOPEFUL. I am sorry that I was so foolish, and am made to wonder that I am not now as Lot's wife; for wherein was

151 Gen. 19:26

the difference betwixt her sin and mine? She only looked back; and I had a desire to go see. Let grace be adored, and let me be ashamed, that ever such a thing should be in mine heart.

CHRISTIAN. Let us take notice of what we see here, for our help for time to come. This woman escaped one judgment, for she fell not by the destruction of Sodom; yet she was destroyed by another, as we see she is turned into a pillar of salt.

HOPEFUL. True, and she may be to us both caution and example; caution, that we should shun her sin; or a sign of what judgment will overtake such as shall not be prevented by this caution; so Korah, Dathan, and Abiram, with the 250 men that perished in their sin, did also become a sign or example to others to beware.[152] But above all, I muse at one thing, to wit, how Demas and his fellows can stand so confidently yonder to look for that treasure, which this woman, but for looking behind her, after (for we read not that she stepped one foot out of the way) was turned into a pillar of salt; especially since the judgment which overtook her did make her an example, within sight of where they are; for they cannot choose but see her, did they but lift up their eyes.

CHRISTIAN. It is a thing to be wondered at, and it argueth that their hearts are grown desperate in the case; and I cannot tell who to compare them to so fitly, as to them that pick pockets in the presence of the judge, or that will out purses under the gallows. It is said of the men of Sodom, that they were sinners exceedingly, because they were sinners before the Lord, that is, in His eyesight, and notwithstanding the kindnesses that He had showed them,[153] for the land

152 Num. 26:9, 10

153 Gen. 13:13

of Sodom was now like the garden of Eden heretofore.[154] This, therefore, provoked Him the more to jealousy, and made their plague as hot as the fire of the Lord out of Heaven could make it. And it is most rationally to be concluded, that such, even such as these are, that shall sin in the sight, yea, and that too in despite of such examples that are set continually before them, to caution them to the contrary, must be partakers of severest judgments.

HOPEFUL. Doubtless thou hast said the truth; but what a mercy is it, that neither thou, but especially I, am not made myself this example! This ministereth occasion to us to thank God, to fear before Him, and always to remember Lot's wife.

I saw, then, that they went on their way to a pleasant river; which David the king called "the river of God," but John "the river of the water of life".[155] Now their way lay just upon the bank of the river; here, therefore, Christian and his companion walked with great delight; they drank also of the water of the river, which was pleasant, and enlivening to their weary spirits: besides, on the banks of this river, on either side, were green trees, that bore all manner of fruit; and the leaves of the trees were good for medicine; with the fruit of these trees they were also much delighted; and the leaves they eat to prevent surfeits, and other diseases that are incident to those that heat their blood by travels. On either side of the river was also a meadow, curiously beautified with lilies, and it was green all the year long. In this meadow they lay down, and slept; for here they might lie down safely. When they awoke, they gathered again of the fruit of the trees, and drank again of the water of the river, and then lay

154 Gen. 13:10

155 Psa. 65:9; Rev. 22; Ezek. 47

down again to sleep.[156] Thus they did several days and nights. Then they sang—

Behold ye how these crystal streams do glide,
To comfort pilgrims by the highway side;
The meadows green, besides their fragrant smell,
Yield dainties for them: and he that can tell
What pleasant fruit, yea, leaves, these trees do yield,
Will soon sell all, that he may buy this field.

So when they were disposed to go on (for they were not, as yet, at their journey's end), they ate and drank, and departed.

Now, I beheld in my dream, that they had not journeyed far, but the river and the way for a time parted; at which they were not a little sorry; yet they durst not go out of the way. Now the way from the river was rough, and their feet tender, by reason of their travels; "so the souls of the pilgrims were much discouraged because of the way".[157] Wherefore, still as they went on, they wished for better way. Now, a little before them, there was on the left hand of the road a meadow, and a stile to go over into it; and that meadow is called By-path Meadow. Then said Christian to his fellow, If this meadow lieth along by our way-side, let us go over into it. Then he went to the stile to see, and behold, a path lay along by the way, on the other side of the fence. It is according to my wish, said Christian. Here is the easiest going; come, good Hopeful, and let us go over.

HOPEFUL. But how if this path should lead us out of the way?

CHRISTIAN. That is not like, said the other. Look, doth it

156 Psa. 23:2; Isa. 14:30
157 Num. 21:4

not go along by the way-side? So Hopeful, being persuaded by his fellow, went after him over the stile. When they were gone over, and were got into the path, they found it very easy for their feet; and withal, they, looking before them, espied a man walking as they did (and his name was Vain-confidence); so they called after him, and asked him whither that way led. He said, to the Celestial Gate. Look, said Christian, did not I tell you so? By this you may see we are right. So they followed, and he went before them. But, behold, the night came on, and it grew very dark; so that they that were behind, lost the sight of him that went before.

He, therefore, that went before (Vain-confidence by name), not seeing the way before him, fell into a deep pit,[158] which was on purpose there made, by the Prince of those grounds, to catch vain-glorious fools withal, and was dashed in pieces with his fall.

Now Christian and his fellow heard him fall. So they called to know the matter, but there was none to answer; only they heard a groaning. Then said Hopeful, Where are we now? Then was his fellow silent, as mistrusting that he had led him out of the way; and now it began to rain, and thunder, and lighten in a very dreadful manner; and the water rose amain.

Then Hopeful groaned in himself, saying, O that I had kept on my way!

CHRISTIAN. Who could have thought that this path should have led us out of the way?

HOPEFUL. I was afraid on it at the very first, and therefore gave you that gentle caution. I would have spoke plainer, but that you are older than I.

CHRISTIAN. Good brother, be not offended; I am sorry I have brought thee out of the way, and that I have put thee

158 Isa. 9:16

into such imminent danger; pray, my brother, forgive me; I did not do it of an evil intent.

HOPEFUL. Be comforted, my brother, for I forgive thee; and believe too that this shall be for our good.

CHRISTIAN. I am glad I have with me a merciful brother; but we must not stand thus: let us try to go back again.

HOPEFUL. But, good brother, let me go before.

CHRISTIAN. No, if you please, let me go first, that if there be any danger, I may be first therein, because by my means we are both gone out of the way.

HOPEFUL. No, said Hopeful, you shall not go first; for your mind being troubled may lead you out of the way again. Then, for their encouragement, they heard the voice of one saying, "Set thine heart toward the highway, even the way which thou wentest; turn again".[159] But by this time the waters were greatly risen, by reason of which the way of going back was very dangerous. (Then I thought that it is easier going out of the way when we are in, than going in when we are out). Yet they adventured to go back, but it was so dark, and the flood was so high, that in their going back they had like to have been drowned nine or 10 times.

Neither could they, with all the skill they had, get again to the stile that night. Wherefore, at last, lighting under a little shelter, they sat down there until the day-break; but, being weary, they fell asleep. Now there was, not far from the place where they lay, a castle, called Doubting Castle, the owner whereof was Giant Despair; and it was in his grounds they now were sleeping: wherefore he, getting up in the morning early, and walking up and down in his fields, caught Christian and Hopeful asleep in his grounds. Then, with a grim and surly voice, he bid them awake; and asked them whence they were, and what they did in his grounds.

159 Jer. 31:21

They told him they were pilgrims, and that they had lost their way. Then said the Giant, You have this night trespassed on me, by trampling in, and lying on my grounds, and therefore you must go along with me. So they were forced to go, because he was stronger than they. They also had but little to say, for they knew themselves in a fault. The Giant therefore drove them before him, and put them into his castle, into a very dark dungeon, nasty and stinking to the spirits of these two men.[160] Here then they lay from Wednesday morning till Saturday night, without one bit of bread, or drop of drink, or light, or any to ask how they did; they were therefore here in evil case, and were far from friends and acquaintance. Now in this place Christian had double sorrow, because it was through his unadvised counsel that they were brought into this distress.

Now, Giant Despair had a wife, and her name was Diffidence. So, when he was gone to bed, he told his wife what he had done; to wit, that he had taken a couple of prisoners, and cast them into his dungeon, for trespassing on his grounds. Then he asked her also what he had best to do further to them. So she asked him what they were, whence they came, and whither they were bound; and he told her. Then she counselled him, that when he arose in the morning he should beat them without any mercy. So, when he arose, he getteth him a grievous crab-tree cudgel, and goes down into the dungeon to them, and there first falls to rating of them as if they were dogs, although they never gave him a word of distaste. Then he falls upon them, and beats them fearfully, in such sort, that they were not able to help themselves, or to turn them upon the floor. This done, he withdraws and leaves them, there to condole their misery, and to mourn under their distress. So all that day they spent the

160 Psa. 88:18

time in nothing but sighs and bitter lamentations. The next night, she, talking with her husband about them further, and understanding that they were yet alive, did advise him to counsel them to make away themselves. So when morning was come, he goes to them in a surly manner as before, and perceiving them to be very sore with the stripes that he had given them the day before, he told them, that since they were never like to come out of that place, their only way would be forthwith to make an end of themselves, either with knife, halter, or poison, for why, said he, should you choose life, seeing it is attended with so much bitterness? But they desired him to let them go. With that he looked ugly upon them, and, rushing to them, had doubtless made an end of them himself, but that he fell into one of his fits (for he sometimes, in sunshiny weather, fell into fits), and lost for a time the use of his hand; wherefore he withdrew, and left them as before, to consider what to do. Then did the prisoners consult between themselves, whether it was best to take his counsel or no; and thus they began to discourse:

CHRISTIAN. Brother, said Christian, what shall we do? The life that we now live is miserable. For my part, I know not whether is best, to live thus, or to die out of hand. "My soul chooseth strangling rather than life," and the grave is more easy for me than this dungeon.[161] Shall we be ruled by the Giant?

HOPEFUL. Indeed, our present condition is dreadful, and death would be far more welcome to me than thus for ever to abide; but yet, let us consider, the Lord of the country to which we are going hath said, Thou shalt do no murder: no, not to another man's person; much more, then, are we forbidden to take his counsel to kill ourselves. Besides, he that kills another, can but commit murder upon his body; but

161 Job 7:15

for one to kill himself, is to kill body and soul at once. And, moreover, my brother, thou talkest of ease in the grave; but hast thou forgotten the hell, whither for certain the murderers go? For "no murderer hath eternal life," etc. And let us consider, again, that all the law is not in the hand of Giant Despair. Others, so far as I can understand, have been taken by him, as well as we; and yet have escaped out of his hand. Who knows, but that God that made the world may cause that Giant Despair may die? or that, at some time or other, he may forget to lock us in? or that he may, in a short time, have another of his fits before us, and may lose the use of his limbs? and if ever that should come to pass again, for my part, I am resolved to pluck up the heart of a man, and to try my utmost to get from under his hand. I was a fool that I did not try to do it before; but, however, my brother, let us be patient, and endure a while. The time may come that may give us a happy release; but let us not be our own murderers. With these words, Hopeful at present did moderate the mind of his brother; so they continued together (in the dark) that day, in their sad and doleful condition.

Well, towards evening, the Giant goes down into the dungeon again, to see if his prisoners had taken his counsel; but when he came there, he found them alive; and truly, alive was all; for now, what for want of bread and water, and by reason of the wounds they received when he beat them, they could do little but breathe. But, I say, he found them alive; at which he fell into a grievous rage, and told them, that seeing they had disobeyed his counsel, it should be worse with them than if they had never been born.

At this they trembled greatly, and I think that Christian fell into a swoon; but, coming a little to himself again, they renewed their discourse about the Giant's counsel, and whether yet they had best to take it or no. Now Christian again seemed to be for doing it, but Hopeful made his second reply as followeth—

HOPEFUL. My brother, said he, rememberest thou not how valiant thou hast been heretofore? Apollyon could not crush thee, nor could all that thou didst hear, or see, or feel, in the Valley of the Shadow of Death. What hardship, terror, and amazement hast thou already gone through! And art thou now nothing but fear! Thou seest that I am in the dungeon with thee, a far weaker man by nature than thou art; also, this Giant has wounded me as well as thee, and hath also cut off the bread and water from my mouth; and with thee I mourn without the light. But let us exercise a little more patience; remember how thou playedst the man at Vanity Fair, and wast neither afraid of the chain, nor cage, nor yet of bloody death. Wherefore let us (at least to avoid the shame, that becomes not a Christian to be found in) bear up with patience as well as we can.

Now, night being come again, and the Giant and his wife being in bed, she asked him concerning the prisoners, and if they had taken his counsel. To which he replied, They are sturdy rogues, they choose rather to bear all hardship, than to make away themselves. Then said she, Take them into the castle-yard tomorrow, and show them the bones and skulls of those that thou hast already despatched, and make them believe, ere a week comes to an end, thou also wilt tear them in pieces, as thou hast done their fellows before them.

So when the morning was come, the Giant goes to them again, and takes them into the castle-yard, and shows them, as his wife had bidden him. These, said he, were pilgrims as you are, once, and they trespassed in my grounds, as you have done; and when I thought fit, I tore them in pieces, and so, within 10 days, I will do you. Go, get you down to your den again; and with that, he beat them all the way thither. They lay, therefore, all day on Saturday in a lamentable case, as before. Now, when night was come, and when Mrs. Diffidence and her husband, the Giant, were got to bed, they began to renew their discourse of their prisoners; and withal the old Giant wondered, that he could neither by his blows nor his counsel bring them to an end. And with that his wife replied, I fear, Said she, that they live in hope that some will come to relieve them, or that they have picklocks about them, by the means of which they hope to escape. And sayest thou so, my dear? said the Giant; I will, therefore, search them in the morning.

Well, on Saturday, about midnight, they began to pray, and continued in prayer till almost break of day.

Now, a little before it was day, good Christian, as one half-amazed, brake out in this passionate speech: What a fool, quoth he, am I, thus to lie in a stinking dungeon, when I may as well walk at liberty! I have a key in my bosom, called Promise, that will, I am persuaded, open any lock in Doubting Castle. Then said Hopeful, That is good news, good brother; pluck it out of thy bosom, and try.

Then Christian pulled it out of his bosom, and began to try at the dungeon door, whose bolt (as he turned the key) gave back, and the door flew open with ease, and Christian and Hopeful both came out. Then he went to the outward door that leads into the castle-yard, and, with his key, opened that door also. After, he went to the iron gate, for that must be opened too; but that lock went damnable hard, yet the key did open it. Then they thrust open the gate to make their escape with speed, but that gate, as it opened, made such a creaking, that it waked Giant Despair, who, hastily rising to pursue his prisoners, felt his limbs to fail, for his fits took him again, so that he could by no means go after them. Then they went on, and came to the King's highway, and so were safe, because they were out of his jurisdiction.

Now, when they were gone over the stile, they began to contrive with themselves what they should do at that stile, to prevent those that should come after, from falling into the hands of Giant Despair. So they consented to erect there a pillar, and to engrave upon the side thereof this sentence—"Over this stile is the way to Doubting Castle, which is kept by Giant Despair, who despiseth the King of the Celestial Country, and seeks to destroy His holy pilgrims." Many, therefore, that followed after, read what was written, and escaped the danger. This done, they sang as follows—

Out of the way we went, and then we found
What 'twas to tread upon forbidden ground;
And let them that come after have a care,
Lest heedlessness makes them, as we, to fare.
Lest they for trespassing his prisoners are,
Whose castle's Doubting, and whose name's Despair.

THE DELECTABLE MOUNTAINS

They went then till they came to the Delectable Mountains, which mountains belong to the Lord of that hill of which we have spoken before; so they went up to the mountains, to behold the gardens and orchards, the vineyards and fountains of water; where also they drank and washed themselves, and did freely eat of the vineyards. Now there were on the tops of these mountains, shepherds feeding their flocks, and they stood by the highway side. The Pilgrims therefore went to them, and leaning upon their staves (as is common with weary pilgrims, when they stand to talk with any by the way), they asked, Whose Delectable Mountains are these? And whose be the sheep that feed upon them?

SHEPHERDS. These mountains are Immanuel's Land, and they are within sight of His city; and the sheep also are His, and He laid down His life for them.[162]

CHRISTIAN. Is this the way to the Celestial City?

SHEPHERDS. You are just in your way.

CHRISTIAN. How far is it thither?

SHEPHERDS. Too far for any but those that shall get thither indeed.

CHRISTIAN. Is the way safe or dangerous?

162 John 10:11

SHEPHERDS. Safe for those for whom it is to be safe; but the transgressors shall fall therein.[163]

CHRISTIAN. Is there, in this place, any relief for pilgrims that are weary and faint in the way?

SHEPHERDS. The Lord of these mountains hath given us a charge not to be "forgetful to entertain strangers";[164] therefore the good of the place is before you.

I saw also in my dream, that when the Shepherds perceived that they were wayfaring men, they also put questions to them, to which they made answer as in other places; as, Whence came you? And, How got you into the way? And, by what means have you so persevered therein? For but few of them that begin to come hither, do show their face on these mountains. But when the Shepherds heard their answers, being pleased therewith, they looked very lovingly upon them, and said, Welcome to the Delectable Mountains.

The Shepherds, I say, whose names were Knowledge, Experience, Watchful, and Sincere, took them by the hand, and had them to their tents, and made them partake of that which was ready at present. They said, moreover, We would that ye should stay here a while, to be acquainted with us; and yet more to solace yourselves with the good of these Delectable Mountains. They then told them that they were content to stay; so they went to their rest that night, because it was very late.

Then I saw in my dream, that in the morning the Shepherds called up Christian and Hopeful to walk with them upon the mountains: so they went forth with them, and walked a while, having a pleasant prospect on every side. Then said the Shepherds one to another, Shall we show these

163 Hosea 14:9

164 Heb. 13:2

Pilgrims some wonders? So when they had concluded to do it, they had them first to the top of a hill Error, which was very steep on the furthest side, and bid them look down to the bottom. So Christian and Hopeful looked down, and saw at the bottom several men dashed all to pieces by a fall that they had from the top. Then said Christian, What meaneth this? The Shepherds answered, Have you not heard of them that were made to err, by hearkening to Hymeneus and Philetus, as concerning the faith of the resurrection of the body?[165] They answered, Yes. Then said the Shepherds, Those that you see lie dashed in pieces at the bottom of this mountain are they; and they have continued to this day unburied, as you see, for an example to others to take heed how they clamber too high, or how they come too near the brink of this mountain.

Then I saw that they had them to the top of another mountain, and the name of that is Caution, and bid them look afar off; which, when they did, they perceived, as they thought, several men walking up and down among the tombs that were there; and they perceived that the men were blind, because they stumbled sometimes upon the tombs, and because they could not get out from among them. Then said Christian, What means this?

The Shepherds then answered, Did you not see a little below these mountains a stile that led into a meadow, on the left hand of this way? They answered, Yes. Then said the Shepherds, From that stile there goes a path that leads directly to Doubting Castle, which is kept by Giant Despair, and these, pointing to them among the tombs, came once on pilgrimage as you do now, even till they came to that same stile; and because the right way was rough in that place, they chose to go out of it into that meadow, and there

165 2 Tim. 2:17, 18

were taken by Giant Despair, and cast into Doubting Castle: where, after they had been a while kept in the dungeon, he at last did put out their eyes, and led them among those tombs, where he has left them to wander to this very day, that the saying of the wise man might be fulfilled, "He that wandereth out of the way of understanding, shall remain in the congregation of the dead".[166] Then Christian and Hopeful looked upon one another, with tears gushing out, but yet said nothing to the Shepherds.

166 Prov. 21:16

CHRISTIAN, HOPEFUL, AND THE SHEPHERDS

Then I saw in my dream, that the Shepherds had them to another place, in a bottom, where was a door in the side of a hill, and they opened the door, and bid them look in. They looked in, therefore, and saw that within it was very dark and smoky; they also thought that they heard there a rumbling noise as of fire, and a cry of some tormented, and that they smelt the scent of brimstone. Then said Christian, What means this? The Shepherds told them, This is a byway to hell, a way that hypocrites go in at; namely, such as sell their birthright, with Esau; such as sell their master, with Judas; such as blaspheme the Gospel, with Alexander; and that lie and dissemble, with Ananias and Sapphira his wife. Then said Hopeful to the Shepherds, I perceive that these had on them, even every one, a show of pilgrimage, as we have now; had they not?

SHEPHERDS. Yes, and held it a long time too.

HOPEFUL. How far might they go on in pilgrimage in their day, since they notwithstanding were thus miserably cast away?

SHEPHERDS. Some further, and some not so far, as these mountains.

Then said the Pilgrims one to another, We had need to cry to the Strong for strength.

SHEPHERDS. Aye, and you will have need to use it, when you have it, too.

By this time the Pilgrims had a desire to go forward, and the Shepherds a desire they should; so they walked together towards the end of the mountains. Then said the Shepherds one to another, Let us here show to the Pilgrims the gates of the Celestial City, if they have skill to look through our perspective glass. The Pilgrims then lovingly accepted the motion; so they had them to the top of a high hill, called Clear, and gave them their glass to look.

Then they essayed to look, but the remembrance of that last thing that the Shepherds had showed them, made their hands shake; by means of which impediment, they could not look steadily through the glass; yet they thought they saw something like the gate, and also some of the glory of the place. Then they went away, and sang this song—

Thus, by the Shepherds, secrets are reveal'd,
Which from all other men are kept conceal'd
Come to the Shepherds, then, if you would see
Things deep, things hid, and that mysterious be.

When they were about to depart, one of the Shepherds gave them a note of the way. Another of them bid them beware of the Flatterer. The third bid them take heed that they sleep not upon the Enchanted Ground. And the fourth bid them God speed. So I awoke from my dream.

And I slept, and dreamed again, and saw the same two Pilgrims going down the mountains along the highway towards the city. Now, a little below these mountains, on the left hand, lieth the country of Conceit; from which country there comes into the way in which the Pilgrims walked, a little crooked lane. Here, therefore, they met with a very brisk lad, that came out of that country; and his name was Ignorance. So Christian asked him from what parts he came, and whither he was going.

IGNORANCE. Sir, I was born in the country that lieth off there, a little on the left hand, and I am going to the Celestial City.

CHRISTIAN. But how do you think to get in at the gate? for you may find some difficulty there.

IGNORANCE. As other good people do, said he.

CHRISTIAN. But what have you to show at that gate, that may cause that the gate should be opened to you?

IGNOR. I know my Lord's will, and I have been a good liver; I pay every man his own; I pray, fast, pay tithes, and give alms, and have left my country for whither I am going.

CHRISTIAN. But thou camest not in at the wicket-gate that is at the head of this way; thou camest in hither through that same crooked lane, and therefore, I fear, however thou mayest think of thyself, when the reckoning day shall come, thou wilt have laid to thy charge that thou art a thief and a robber, instead of getting admittance into the city.

IGNORANCE. Gentlemen, ye be utter strangers to me, I know you not; be content to follow the religion of your country, and I will follow the religion of mine. I hope all will be well. And as for the gate that you talk of, all the world knows that that is a great way off of our country. I cannot think that any man in all our parts doth so much as know the way to it, nor need they matter whether they do or no, since we have, as you see, a fine pleasant green lane, that comes down from our country, the next way into the way.

When Christian saw that the man was "wise in his own conceit," he said to Hopeful, whisperingly, "There is more hope of a fool than of him".[167] And said, moreover, "When he that is a fool walketh by the way, his wisdom faileth him,

167 Prov. 26:12

and he saith to everyone that he is a fool" (Eccl. 10:3). What, shall we talk further with him, or out-go him at present, and so leave him to think of what he hath heard already, and then stop again for him afterwards, and see if by degrees we can do any good to him? Then said Hopeful—

Let Ignorance a little while now muse
On what is said, and let him not refuse
Good counsel to embrace, lest he remain
Still ignorant of what's the chiefest gain.
God saith, those that no understanding have,
Although He made them, them He will not save.

HOPEFUL. He further added, It is not good, I think, to say all to him at once; let us pass him by, if you will, and talk to him anon, even as he is able to bear it.

So they both went on, and Ignorance he came after. Now when they had passed him a little way, they entered into a very dark lane, where they met a man whom seven devils had bound with seven strong cords, and were carrying of him back to the door that they saw on the side of the hill.[168] Now good Christian began to tremble, and so did Hopeful his companion; yet as the devils led away the man, Christian looked to see if he knew him; and he thought it might be one Turn-away, that dwelt in the town of Apostasy. But he did not perfectly see his face, for he did hang his head like a thief that is found. But being once past, Hopeful looked after him, and espied on his back a paper with this inscription, "Wanton professor, and damnable apostate." Then said Christian to his fellow, Now I call to remembrance, that which was told me of a thing that happened to a good man hereabout. The name of the man was Little-faith, but a good

168 Matt. 12:45; Prov. 5:22

man, and he dwelt in the town of Sincere. The thing was this: At the entering in at this passage, there comes down from Broad-way Gate, a lane called Dead Man's Lane; so called because of the murders that are commonly done there; and this Little-faith going on pilgrimage, as we do now, chanced to sit down there, and slept. Now there happened, at that time, to come down the lane from Broad-way Gate, three sturdy rogues, and their names were Faint-heart, Mistrust, and Guilt (three brothers), and they espying Little-faith, where he was, came galloping up with speed. Now the good man was just awake from his sleep, and was getting up to go on his journey. So they came up all to him, and with threatening language bid him stand. At this, Little-faith looked as white as a cloud, and had neither power to fight nor fly. Then said Faint-heart, Deliver thy purse. But he making no haste to do it (for he was loath to lose his money), Mistrust ran up to him, and thrusting his hand into his pocket, pulled out thence a bag of silver. Then he cried out, Thieves! Thieves! With that, Guilt, with a great club that was in his hand, struck Little-faith on the head, and with that blow felled him flat to the ground; where be lay bleeding as one that would bleed to death. All this while the thieves stood by. But, at last, they hearing that some were upon the road, and fearing lest it should be one Great-grace, that dwells in the city of good-confidence, they betook themselves to their heels, and left this good man to shift for himself. Now, after a while, Little-faith came to himself, and getting up, made shift to scrabble on his way. This was the story.

HOPEFUL. But did they take from him all that ever he had?

CHRISTIAN. No; the place where his jewels were they never ransacked, so those he kept still. But, as I was told, the good man was much afflicted for his loss, for the thieves got most of his spending-money. That which they got not (as I said) were jewels, also he had a little odd money left, but scarce enough to bring him to his journey's end;[169] nay, if I were not misinformed, he was forced to beg as be went, to keep himself alive; for his jewels he might not sell. But beg, and do what he could, he went (as we say) with many a hungry belly the most part of the rest of the way.

HOPEFUL. But is it not a wonder they got not from him his certificate, by which he was to receive his admittance at the Celestial Gate?

CHRISTIAN. It is a wonder; but they got not that, though they missed it not through any good cunning of his; for he, being dismayed with their coming upon him, had neither power nor skill to hide anything; so it was more by good Providence than by his endeavour, that they missed of that good thing.

HOPEFUL. But it must needs be a comfort to him, that they got not this jewel from him.

CHRISTIAN. It might have been great comfort to him, had he used it as he should; but they that told me the story said, that he made but little use of it all the rest of the way, and that because of the dismay that he had in the taking away his money; indeed, he forgot it a great part of the rest of his journey; and besides, when at any time it came into his mind, and he began to be comforted therewith, then would fresh thoughts of his loss come again upon him, and those thoughts would swallow up all.[170]

HOPEFUL. Alas! poor man. This could not but be a great grief to him.

CHRISTIAN. Grief! aye, a grief indeed. Would it not have been so to any of us, had we been used as he, to be robbed, and wounded too, and that in a strange place, as he was? It

169 1 Peter 4:18

170 1 Peter 1:9

is a wonder he did not die with grief, poor heart! I was told that he scattered almost all the rest of the way with nothing but doleful and bitter complaints; telling also to all that overtook him, or that he overtook in the way as he went, where he was robbed, and how; who they were that did it, and what he lost; how he was wounded, and that he hardly escaped with his life.

HOPEFUL. But it is a wonder that his necessity did not put him upon selling or pawning some of his jewels, that he might have wherewith to relieve himself in his journey.

CHRISTIAN. Thou talkest like one upon whose head is the shell to this very day; for what should he pawn them, or to whom should he sell them? In all that country where he was robbed, his jewels were not accounted of; nor did he want that relief which could from thence be administered to him. Besides, had his jewels been missing at the gate of the Celestial City, he had (and that he knew well enough) been excluded from an inheritance there; and that would have been worse to him than the appearance and villany of 10,000 thieves.

HOPEFUL. Why art thou so tart, my brother? Esau sold his birthright, and that for a mess of pottage, and that birthright was his greatest jewel; and if he, why might not Little-faith do so too?[171]

CHRISTIAN. Esau did sell his birthright indeed, and so do many besides, and by so doing exclude themselves from the chief blessing, as also that caitiff did; but you must put a difference betwixt Esau and Little-faith, and also betwixt their estates. Esau's birthright was typical, but Little-faith's jewels were not so; Esau's belly was his god, but Little-faith's belly was not so; Esau's want lay in his fleshly appetite, Little-faith's did not so. Besides, Esau could see no further than

171 Heb. 12:16

to the fulfilling of his lusts; "Behold I am at the point to die (said he), and what profit shall this birthright do me?"[172] But Little-faith, though it was his lot to have but a little faith, was by his little faith kept from such extravagances, and made to see and prize his jewels more than to sell them, as Esau did his birthright. You read not anywhere that Esau had faith, no, not so much as a little; therefore no marvel if, where the flesh only bears sway (as it will in that man where no faith is to resist), if he sells his birthright, and his soul and all, and that to the devil of hell; for it is with such, as it is with the ass, who in her occasions cannot be turned away.[173] When their minds are set upon their lusts, they will have them whatever they cost. But Little-faith was of another temper, his mind was on things divine; his livelihood was upon things that were spiritual, and from above; therefore, to what end should he that is of such a temper sell his jewels (had there been any that would have bought them) to fill his mind with empty things? Will a man give a penny to fill his belly with hay; or can you persuade the turtle-dove to live upon carrion like the crow? Though faithless ones can, for carnal lusts, pawn, or mortgage, or sell what they have, and themselves outright to boot; yet they that have faith, saving faith, though but a little of it, cannot do so. Here, therefore, my brother, is thy mistake.

HOPEFUL. I acknowledge it; but yet your severe reflection had almost made me angry.

CHRISTIAN. Why, I did but compare thee to some of the birds that are of the brisker sort, who will run to and fro in untrodden paths, with the shell upon their heads; but pass by that, and consider the matter under debate, and all shall be well betwixt thee and me.

172 Gen. 25:32
173 Jer. 2:24

HOPEFUL. But, Christian, these three fellows, I am persuaded in my heart, are but a company of cowards; would they have run else, think you, as they did, at the noise of one that was coming on the road? Why did not Little-faith pluck up a greater heart? He might, methinks, Have stood one brush with them, and have yielded when there had been no remedy.

CHRISTIAN. That they are cowards, many have said, but few have found it so in the time of trial. As for a great heart, Littlefaith had none; and I perceive by thee, my brother, hadst thou been the man concerned, thou art but for a brush, and then to yield. And, verily, since this is the height of thy stomach, now they are at a distance from us, should they appear to thee as they did to him, they might put thee to second thoughts.

But, consider again, they are but journeymen thieves, they serve under the king of the bottomless pit, who, if need be, will come in to their aid himself, and his voice is as the roaring of a lion.[174] I myself have been engaged as this Little-faith was, and I found it a terrible thing. These three villains set upon me, and I beginning, like a Christian, to resist, they gave but a call, and in came their master. I would, as the saying is, have given my life for a penny; but that, as God would have it, I was clothed with armour of proof. Aye, and yet, though I was so harnessed, I found it hard work to quit myself like a man. No man can tell what in that combat attends us, but he that hath been in the battle himself.

HOPEFUL. Well, but they ran, you see, when they did but suppose that one Great-grace was in the way.

CHRISTIAN. True, they have often fled, both they and their master, when Great-grace hath but appeared; and no marvel; for he is the King's Champion. But, I trow, you

174 Psa. 7:2; 1 Pet. 5:8

will put some difference betwixt Little-faith and the King's Champion. All the King's subjects are not His champions, nor can they, when tried, do such feats of war as he. Is it meet to think that a little child should handle Goliath as David did? Or that there should be the strength of an ox in a wren? Some are strong, some are weak; some have great faith, some have little. This man was one of the weak, and therefore he went to the wall.

HOPEFUL. I would it had been Great-grace for their sakes.

CHRISTIAN. If it had been, he might have had his hands full; for I must tell you, that though Great-grace is excellent good at his weapons, and has, and can, so long as be keeps them at sword's point, do well enough with them; yet, if they get within him, even Faint-heart, Mistrust, or the other, it shall go hard but they will throw up his heels. And when a man is down, you know, what can he do?

Whoso looks well upon Great-grace's face, shall see those scars and cuts there, that shall easily give demonstration of what I say. Yea, once I heard that he should say (and that when he was in the combat), "We despaired even of life." How did these sturdy rogues and their fellows make David groan, mourn, and roar? Yea, Heman and Hezekiah, too, though champions in their day, were forced to bestir them, when by these assaulted; and yet, notwithstanding, they had their coats soundly brushed by them. Peter, upon a time, would go try what he could do; but though some do say of him that he is the prince of the apostles, they handled him so, that they made him at last afraid of a sorry girl.

Besides, their king is at their whistle. He is never out of hearing; and if at any time they be put to the worst, he, if possible, comes in to help them; and of him it is said, "The sword of him that layeth at him cannot hold; the spear, the dart, nor the habergeon: he esteemeth iron as straw, and brass as rotten wood. The arrow cannot make him flee; sling stones are turned with him into stubble. Darts are counted as stubble: he laugheth at the shaking of a spear"[175] What can a man do in this case? It is true, if a man could, at every turn, have Job's horse, and had skill and courage to ride him, he might do notable things; "for his neck is clothed with thunder, he will not be afraid of the grasshopper; the glory of his nostrils is terrible; he paweth in the valley, and rejoiceth in his strength, he goeth on to meet the armed men. He mocketh at fear, and is not affrighted, neither turneth he back from the sword. The quiver rattleth against him, the glittering spear, and the shield. He swalloweth the ground with fierceness and rage, neither believeth he that it is the sound of the trumpet. He saith among the trumpets, Ha, ha! and he smelleth the battle afar off, the thunder of the captains, and the shouting"[176]

But for such footmen as thee and I are, let us never desire to meet with an enemy, nor vaunt as if we could do better, when we hear of others that they have been toiled, nor be tickled at the thoughts of our own manhood; for such commonly come by the worst when tried. Witness Peter, of whom I made mention before. He would swagger, aye, he would; he would, as his vain mind prompted him to say, do better, and stand more for his Master than all men; but who so foiled, and run down by these villains, as he?

When, therefore, we hear that such robberies are done on the King's highway, two things become us to do:

1. To go out harnessed, and to be sure to take a shield with us; for it was for want of that, that he that laid so lustily at Leviathan could not make him yield; for, indeed, if that be wanting, he fears us not at all. Therefore, he that had skill

175 Job. 12:16–19
176 Job 34:16–25

hath said, "Above all, taking the shield of faith, wherewith ye shall be able to quench all the fiery darts of the wicked"[177]

2. It is good, also, that we desire of the King a convoy, yea, that he will go with us Himself. This made David rejoice when in the Valley of the Shadow of Death; and Moses was rather for dying where he stood, than to go one step without his God.[178] O my brother, if He will but go along with us, what need we be afraid of ten thousands that shall set themselves against us?[179] But, without Him, the proud helpers "fall under the slain"[180]

I, for my part, have been in the fray before now; and though, through the goodness of Him that is best, I am, as you see, alive; yet I cannot boast of my manhood: Glad shall I be, if I meet with no more such brunts; though, I fear, we are not got beyond all danger. However, since the lion and the bear have not as yet devoured me, I hope God will also deliver us from the next uncircumcised Philistine. Then sang Christian—

Poor Little-faith! Hast been among the thieves?
Wast robb'd? Remember this, whoso believes,
And gets more faith, shall then a victor be
Over ten thousand, else scarce over three.

So they went on, and Ignorance followed. They went then till they came at a place where they saw a way put itself into their way, and seemed withal to lie as straight as the way which they should go; and here they knew not which of the two to take, for both seemed straight before them;

177 Eph. 6:16
178 Exo. 33:15
179 Psa. 3:5–8; 27:1–3
180 Isa. 10:4

therefore, here they stood still to consider. And as they were thinking about the way, behold a man, black of flesh, but covered with a very light robe, came to them, and asked them why they stood there. They answered, they were going to the Celestial City, but knew not which of these ways to take. Follow me, said the man, it is thither that I am going. So they followed him in the way that but now came into the road, which by degrees turned, and turned them so from the city that they desired to go to, that, in little time, their faces were turned away from it; yet they followed him. But by and by, before they were aware, he led them both within the compass of a net, in which they were both so entangled, that they knew not what to do; and with that the white robe fell off the black man's back. Then they saw where they were. Wherefore, there they lay crying some time, for they could not get themselves out.

CHRISTIAN. Then said Christian to his fellow, Now do I see myself in an error. Did not the Shepherds bid us beware of the flatterers? As is the saying of the wise man, so we have found it this day, "A man that flattereth his neighbour, spreadeth a net for his feet"[181]

HOPEFUL. They also gave us a note of directions about the way, for our more sure finding thereof; but therein we have also forgotten to read, and have not kept ourselves from the paths of the destroyer. Here David was wiser than we; for, saith he, "Concerning the works of men, by the word of thy lips, I have kept me from the paths of the destroyer"[182] Thus they lay bewailing themselves in the net. At last they espied a Shining One coming towards them, with a whip of small cord in his hand. When he was come to the place where they were, he asked them whence they came,

181 Prov. 29:5
182 Psa. 16:4

and what they did there. They told him that they were poor pilgrims going to Zion, but were led out of their way by a black man, clothed in white, who bid us, said they, follow him, for he was going thither too. Then said he with the whip, It is Flatterer, a false apostle, that hath transformed himself into an angel of light.[183] So he rent the net, and let the men out. Then said he to them, Follow me, that I may set you in your way again. So he led them back to the way which they had left to follow the Flatterer. Then he asked them, saying, Where did you lie the last night? They said, With the Shepherds, upon the Delectable Mountains. He asked them then, if they had not of those Shepherds a note of direction for the way. They answered, Yes. But did you, said he, when you were at a stand, pluck out and read your note? They answered, No. He asked them, Why? They said, they forgot. He asked, moreover, if the Shepherds did not bid them beware of the Flatterer. They answered, Yes, but we did not imagine, said they, that this fine-spoken man had been he.[184]

Then I saw in my dream, that he commanded them to lie down; which, when they did, he chastised them sore, to teach them the good way wherein they should walk;[185] and as he chastised them, he said, "As many as I love, I rebuke and chasten; be zealous, therefore, and repent".[186] This done, he bid them go on their way, and take good heed to the other directions of the Shepherds. So they thanked him for all his kindness, and went softly along the right way, singing—

Come hither, you that walk along the way;

183 Prov. 29:5; Dan. 11:32; 2 Cor. 11:13, 14

184 Rom. 16:18

185 Deut. 25:2

186 Rev. 3:19; 2 Chron. 6:26, 27

See how the pilgrims fare that go astray!
They catched are in an entangling net,
'Cause they good counsel lightly did forget:
'Tis true, they rescued were, but yet you see,
They're scourg'd to boot. Let this your caution be.

Now, after a while, they perceived, afar off, one coming softly and alone, all along the highway to meet them. Then said Christian to his fellow, Yonder is a man with his back toward Zion, and he is coming to meet us.

HOPEFUL. I see him, let us take heed to ourselves now, lest he should prove a flatterer also. So he drew nearer and nearer, and at last came up unto them. His name was Atheist, and he asked them whither they were going.

CHRISTIAN. We are going to the Mount Zion.

Then Atheist fell into a very great laughter.

CHRISTIAN. What is the meaning of your laughter?

ATHEIST. I laugh to see what ignorant persons you are, to take upon you so tedious a journey, and yet are like to have nothing but your travel for your pains.

CHRISTIAN. Why, man, do you think we shall not be received?

ATHEIST. Received! There is no such place as you dream of in all this world.

CHRISTIAN. But there is in the world to come.

ATHEIST. When I was at home in mine own country, I heard as you now affirm, and from that hearing went out to see, and have been seeking this city this 20 years; but find no more of it than I did the first day I set out.[187]

CHRISTIAN. We have both heard and believe that there is such a place to be found.

ATHEIST. Had not I, when at home, believed, I had not

187 Jer. 22:12; Eccl. 10:15

come thus far to seek; but finding none (and yet I should, had there been such a place to be found, for I have gone to seek it further than you), I am going back again, and will seek to refresh myself with the things that I then cast away, for hopes of that which, I now see, is not.

CHRISTIAN. Then said Christian to Hopeful his fellow, Is it true which this man hath said?

HOPEFUL. Take heed, he is one of the flatterers; remember what it hath cost us once already for our hearkening to such kind of fellows. What! no Mount Zion? Did we not see, from the Delectable Mountains, the gate of the city? Also, are we not now to walk by faith? Let us go on, said Hopeful, lest the man with the whip overtake us again.[188]

You should have taught me that lesson, which I will round you in the ears withal: "Cease, my son, to hear the instruction that causeth to err from the words of knowledge".[189] I say, my brother, cease to hear him, and let us "believe to the saving of the soul".[190]

CHRISTIAN. My brother, I did not put the question to thee, for that I doubted of the truth of our belief myself, but to prove thee, and to fetch from thee a fruit of the honesty of thy heart. As for this man, I know that he is blinded by the god of this world. Let thee and I go on, knowing that we have belief of the truth, "and no lie is of the truth"[191]

HOPEFUL. Now do I rejoice in hope of the glory of God. So they turned away from the man; and he, laughing at them, went his way.

188 2 Cor. 5:7

189 Prov. 19:17

190 Heb. 10:39

191 1 John 2:21

ADVENTURES ON THE ENCHANTED GROUND

I saw then in my dream, that they went till they came into a certain country, whose air naturally tended to make one drowsy, if he came a stranger into it. And here Hopeful began to be very dull and heavy of sleep; wherefore he said unto Christian, I do now begin to grow so drowsy that I can scarcely hold up mine eyes; let us lie down here, and take one nap.

CHRISTIAN. By no means, said the other; lest, sleeping, we never awake more.

HOPEFUL. Why, my brother? Sleep is sweet to the labouring man; we may be refreshed if we take a nap.

CHRISTIAN. Do you not remember that one of the Shepherds bid us beware of the Enchanted Ground? He meant by that, that we should beware of sleeping; "Therefore let us not sleep, as do others, but let us watch and be sober"[192]

HOPEFUL. I acknowledge myself in a fault; and had I been here alone, I had by sleeping run the danger of death. I see it is true that the wise man saith, "Two are better than

192 1 Thess. 5:6

one." Hitherto hath thy company been my mercy, and thou shalt have a good reward for thy labour.[193]

CHRISTIAN. Now then, said Christian, to prevent drowsiness in this place, let us fall into good discourse.

HOPEFUL. With all my heart, said the other.

CHRISTIAN. Where shall we begin?

HOPEFUL. Where God began with us. But do you begin, if you please.

CHRISTIAN. I will sing you first this song—

When saints do sleepy grow, let them come hither,
And hear how these two pilgrims talk together:
Yea, let them learn of them, in any wise,
Thus to keep ope their drowsy slumb'ring eyes.
Saints' fellowship, if it be manag'd well,
Keeps them awake, and that in spite of hell.

CHRISTIAN. Then Christian began, and said, I will ask you a question. How came you to think at first of so doing as you do now?

HOPEFUL. Do you mean, how came I at first to look after the good of my soul?

CHRISTIAN. Yes, that is my meaning.

HOPEFUL. I continued a great while in the delight of those things which were seen and sold at our fair; things which, I believe now, would have, had I continued in them still, drowned me in perdition and destruction.

CHRISTIAN. What things were they?

HOPEFUL. All the treasures and riches of the world. Also I delighted much in rioting, revelling, drinking, swearing, lying, uncleanness, Sabbath-breaking, and what not, that tended to destroy the soul. But I found at last, by hearing

193 Eccl. 4:9

and considering of things that are Divine, which indeed I heard of you, as also of beloved Faithful, that was put to death for his faith and good living in Vanity Fair, that "the end of these things is death"[194] And that for these things' sake, "cometh the wrath of God upon the children of disobedience"[195]

CHRISTIAN. And did you presently fall under the power of this conviction?

HOPEFUL. No, I was not willing presently to know the evil of sin, nor the damnation that follows upon the commission of it; but endeavoured, when my mind at first began to be shaken with the Word, to shut mine eyes against the light thereof.

CHRISTIAN. But what was the cause of your carrying of it thus to the first workings of God's blessed Spirit upon you?

HOPEFUL. The causes were, 1. I was ignorant that this was the work of God upon me. I never thought that by awakenings for sin, God at first begins the conversion of a sinner. 2. Sin was yet very sweet to my flesh, and I was loath to leave it. 3. I could not tell how to part with mine old companions, their presence and actions were so desirable unto me. 4. The hours in which convictions were upon me, were such troublesome and such heart-affrighting hours, that I could not bear, no not so much as the remembrance of them upon my heart.

CHRISTIAN. Then, as it seems, sometimes you got rid of your trouble?

HOPEFUL. Yes, verily, but it would come into my mind again, and then I should be as bad, nay, worse than I was before.

194 Rev. 6:12–13

195 Eph. 5:6

CHRISTIAN. Why, what was it that brought your sins to mind again?

HOPEFUL. Many things; as,

1. If I did but meet a good man in the streets; or,

2. If I have heard any read in the Bible; or,

3. If mine head did begin to ache; or,

4. If I were told that some of my neighbours were sick; or,

5. If I heard the bell toll for some that were dead; or,

6. If I thought of dying myself; or,

7. If I heard that sudden death happened to others;

8. But especially, when I thought of myself, that I must quickly come to judgment.

CHRISTIAN. And could you at any time, with ease, get off the guilt of sin, when, by any of these ways, it came upon you?

HOPEFUL. No, not I, for then they got faster hold of my conscience; and then, if I did but think of going back to sin (though my mind was turned against it), it would be double torment to me.

CHRISTIAN. And how did you do then?

HOPEFUL. I thought I must endeavour to mend my life; for else, thought I, I am sure to be damned.

CHRISTIAN. And did you endeavour to mend?

HOPEFUL. Yes; and fled from not only my sins, but sinful company too; and betook me to religious duties, as prayer, reading, weeping for sin, speaking truth to my neighbours, etc. These things did I, with many others, too much here to relate.

CHRISTIAN. And did you think yourself well then?

HOPEFUL. Yes, for a while; but, at the last, my trouble came tumbling upon me again, and that over the neck of all my reformations.

CHRISTIAN. How came that about, since you were now reformed?

HOPEFUL. There were several things brought it upon me, especially such sayings as these: "All our righteousnesses are as filthy rags".[196] "By the works of the law shall no flesh be justified".[197] "When ye shall have done all those things, say, We are unprofitable";[198] with many more such like. From whence I began to reason with myself thus: If ALL my righteousnesses are filthy rags; if, by the deeds of the law, NO man can be justified; and if, when we have done ALL, we are yet unprofitable, then it is but a folly to think of Heaven by the law. I further thought thus: If a man runs a hundred pounds into the shopkeeper's debt, and after that shall pay for all that he shall fetch; yet, if this old debt stands still in the book uncrossed, for that the shopkeeper may sue him, and cast him into prison till he shall pay the debt.

CHRISTIAN. Well, and how did you apply this to yourself?

HOPEFUL. Why, I thought thus with myself: I have, by my sins, run a great way into God's book, and that my now reforming will not pay off that score; therefore I should think still, under all my present amendments, But how shall I be freed from that damnation that I have brought myself in danger of, by my former transgressions?

CHRISTIAN. A very good application; but, pray, go on.

HOPEFUL. Another thing that hath troubled me, even since my late amendments, is, that if I look narrowly into the best of what I do now, I still see sin, new sin, mixing itself with the best of that I do; so that now I am forced to conclude, that notwithstanding my former fond conceits of

196 Isa. 64:6

197 Gal. 2:16

198 Luke 17:10

myself and duties, I have committed sin enough in one duty to send me to hell, though my former life had been faultless.

CHRISTIAN. And what did you do then?

HOPEFUL. Do! I could not tell what to do, until I brake my mind to Faithful, for he and I were well acquainted. And he told me, that unless I could obtain the righteousness of a man that never had sinned, neither mine own, nor all the righteousness of the world, could save me.

CHRISTIAN. And did you think he spake true?

HOPEFUL. Had he told me so when I was pleased and satisfied with mine own amendment, I had called him fool for his pains; but now, since I see mine own infirmity, and the sin that cleaves to my best performance, I have been forced to be of his opinion.

CHRISTIAN. But did you think, when at first he suggested it to you, that there was such a man to be found, of whom it might justly be said, that He never committed sin?

HOPEFUL. I must confess the words at first sounded strangely, but after a little more talk and company with him, I had full conviction about it.

CHRISTIAN. And did you ask him what man this was, and how you must be justified by Him?

HOPEFUL. Yes, and he told me it was the Lord Jesus, that dwelleth on the right hand of the Most High. And thus, said he, you must be justified by Him, even by trusting to what He hath done by Himself in the days of His flesh, and suffered when He did hang on the tree. I asked him further, how that man's righteousness could be of that efficacy to justify another before God? And he told me He was the mighty God, and did what He did, and died the death also, not for Himself, but for me; to whom His doings, and the worthiness of them, should be imputed, if I believed on Him.[199]

199 Heb. 10; Rom. 4; Col. 1; 1 Peter 1

CHRISTIAN. And what did you do then?

HOPEFUL. I made my objections against my believing, for that I thought He was not willing to save me.

CHRISTIAN. And what said Faithful to you then?

HOPEFUL. He bid me go to Him and see. Then I said it was presumption; but he said, No, for I was invited to come.[200] Then he gave me a book of Jesus, His inditing, to encourage me the more freely to come; and he said, concerning that book, that every jot and tittle thereof stood firmer than Heaven and earth.[201] Then I asked him, What I must do when I came; and he told me, I must entreat upon my knees, with all my heart and soul, the Father to reveal Him to me.[202] Then I asked him further, how I must make my supplication to Him? And he said, Go, and thou shalt find Him upon a mercy-seat, where He sits all the year long, to give pardon and forgiveness to them that come. I told him that I knew not what to say when I came. And he bid me say to this effect, God be merciful to me a sinner, and make me to know and believe in Jesus Christ; for I see, that if His righteousness had not been, or I have not faith in that righteousness, I am utterly cast away. Lord, I have heard that Thou art a merciful God, and hast ordained that Thy Son Jesus Christ should be the Saviour of the world; and moreover, that thou art willing to bestow Him upon such a poor sinner as I am (and I am a sinner indeed), Lord, take therefore this opportunity, and magnify Thy grace in the salvation of my soul, through Thy Son Jesus Christ. Amen.[203]

CHRISTIAN. And did you do as you were bidden?

HOPEFUL. Yes; over, and over, and over.

200 Matt. 11:28

201 Matt. 24:35

202 Psa. 95:6; Dan. 6:10; Jer. 29:12, 13

203 Exo. 25:22; Lev. 16:2; Num. 7:89; Heb. 4:16

CHRISTIAN. And did the Father reveal His Son to you?

HOPEFUL. Not at the first, nor second, nor third, nor fourth, nor fifth; no, nor at the sixth time neither.

CHRISTIAN. What did you do then?

HOPEFUL. What! why I could not tell what to do.

CHRISTIAN. Had you not thoughts of leaving off praying?

HOPEFUL. Yes, a hundred times twice told.

CHRISTIAN. And what was the reason you did not?

HOPEFUL. I believed that that was true which had been told me, to wit, that without the righteousness of this Christ, all the world could not save me; and therefore, thought I with myself, if I leave off I die, and I can but die at the throne of grace. And withal, this came into my mind, "Though it tarry, wait for it; because it will surely come, it will not tarry".[204] So I continued praying until the Father showed me His Son.

CHRISTIAN. And how was He revealed unto you?

HOPEFUL. I did not see Him with my bodily eyes, but with the eyes of my understanding;[205] and thus it was: One day I was very sad, I think sadder than at any one time in my life, and this sadness was through a fresh sight of the greatness and vileness of my sins. And as I was then looking for nothing but hell, and the everlasting damnation of my soul, suddenly, as I thought, I saw the Lord Jesus look down from Heaven upon me, and saying, "Believe on the Lord Jesus Christ, and thou shalt be saved".[206]

But I replied, Lord, I am a great, a very great sinner. And He answered, "My grace is sufficient for thee".[207] Then

204 Hab. 2:3
205 Eph. 1:18, 19
206 Acts 16:31
207 2 Cor. 12:9

I said, But, Lord, what is believing? And then I saw from that saying, "He that cometh to Me shall never hunger, and he that believeth on Me shall never thirst"; that believing and coming was all one; and that he that came, that is, ran out in his heart and affections after salvation by Christ, he indeed believed in Christ.[208] Then the water stood in mine eyes, and I asked further, But, Lord, may such a great sinner as I am, be indeed accepted of Thee, and be saved by Thee? And I heard him say, "And him that cometh to Me, I will in no wise cast out".[209] Then I said, But how, Lord, must I consider of Thee in my coming to Thee, that my faith may be placed aright upon Thee? Then He said, "Christ Jesus came into the world to save sinners".[210] "He is the end of the law for righteousness to every one that believeth".[211] "He died for our sins, and rose again for our justification".[212] "He loved us, and washed us from our sins in His own blood".[213] "He is mediator betwixt God and us".[214] "He ever liveth to make intercession for us".[215] From all which I gathered, that I must look for righteousness in His person, and for satisfaction for my sins by His blood; that what He did in obedience to His Father's law, and in submitting to the penalty thereof, was not for Himself, but for him that will accept it for his salvation, and be thankful. And now was my heart full of joy, mine eyes full of tears, and mine affections running over with love to the name, people, and ways of Jesus Christ.

CHRISTIAN. This was a revelation of Christ to your soul

208 John 6:35
209 John 6:37
210 1 Tim. 1:15
211 Rom. 10:4
212 Rom. 4:25
213 Rev. 1:5
214 1 Tim. 2:5
215 Heb. 7:25

indeed; but tell me particularly what effect this had upon your spirit.

HOPEFUL. It made me see that all the world, notwithstanding all the righteousness thereof, is in a state of condemnation. It made me see that God the Father, though He be just, can justly justify the coming sinner. It made me greatly ashamed of the vileness of my former life, and confounded me with the sense of mine own ignorance; for there never came thought into my heart before now, that showed me so the beauty of Jesus Christ. It made me love a holy life, and long to do something for the honour and glory of the name of the Lord Jesus; yea, I thought that had I now a thousand gallons of blood in my body, I could spill it all for the sake of the Lord Jesus.

I saw then in my dream that Hopeful looked back and saw Ignorance, whom they had left behind, coming after. Look, said he to Christian, how far yonder youngster loitereth behind.

CHRISTIAN. Aye, aye, I see him; he careth not for our company.

HOPEFUL. But I trow it would not have hurt him, had he kept pace with us hitherto.

CHRISTIAN. That is true; but I warrant you he thinketh otherwise.

HOPEFUL. That I think he doth; but, however, let us tarry for him. So they did.

Then Christian said to him, Come away, man, why do you stay so behind?

IGNORANCE. I take my pleasure in walking alone, even more a great deal than in company, unless I like it the better.

Then said Christian to Hopeful (but softly), Did I not tell you he cared not for our company? But, however, said he, come up, and let us talk away the time in this solitary place. Then, directing his speech to Ignorance, he said,

Come, how do you? How stands it between God and your soul now?

IGNORANCE. I hope well; for I am always full of good motions, that come into my mind, to comfort me as I walk.[216]

CHRISTIAN. What good motions? pray, tell us.

IGNORANCE. Why, I think of God and Heaven.

CHRISTIAN. So do the devils and damned souls.

IGNORANCE. But I think of them, and desire them.

CHRISTIAN. So do many that are never like to come there. "The soul of the sluggard desireth, and hath nothing".[217]

IGNORANCE. But I think of them, and leave all for them.

CHRISTIAN. That I doubt; for leaving all is a hard matter; yea, a harder matter than many are aware of. But why, or by what, art thou persuaded that thou hast left all for God and Heaven?

IGNORANCE. My heart tells me so.

CHRISTIAN. The wise man says, "He that trusts his own heart is a fool".[218]

IGNORANCE. This is spoken of an evil heart, but mine is a good one.

CHRISTIAN. But how dost thou prove that?

IGNORANCE. It comforts me in hopes of Heaven.

CHRISTIAN. That may be through its deceitfulness; for a man's heart may minister comfort to him in the hopes of that thing, for which he yet has no ground to hope.

IGNORANCE. But my heart and life agree together, and therefore my hope is well grounded.

216 Prov. 28:26

217 Prov. 13:4

218 Prov. 28:26

CHRISTIAN. Who told thee that thy heart and life agree together?

IGNORANCE. My heart tells me so.

CHRISTIAN. Ask my fellow if I be a thief! Thy heart tells thee so! Except the Word of God beareth witness in this matter, other testimony is of no value.

IGNOR. But is it not a good heart that hath good thoughts? and is not that a good life that is according to God's commandments?

CHRISTIAN. Yea, that is a good heart that hath good thoughts, and that is a good life that is according to God's commandments; but it is one thing, indeed, to have these, and another thing only to think so.

IGNORANCE. Pray, what count you good thoughts, and a life according to God's commandments?

CHRISTIAN. There are good thoughts of divers kinds; some respecting ourselves, some God, some Christ, and some other thing.

IGNORANCE. What be good thoughts respecting ourselves?

CHRISTIAN. Such as agree with the Word of God.

IGNORANCE. When do our thoughts of ourselves agree with the Word of God?

CHRISTIAN. When we pass the same judgment upon ourselves which the Word passes. To explain myself—the Word of God saith of persons in a natural condition, "There is none righteous, there is none that doeth good".[219] It saith also, that "every imagination of the heart of man is only evil, and that continually".[220] And again, "The imagination of man's heart is evil from his youth".[221] Now then, when we

219 Rom. 3

220 Gen. 6:5

221 Gen. 8:21

think thus of ourselves, having sense thereof then are our thoughts good ones, because according to the Word of God.

IGNORANCE. I will never believe that my heart is thus bad.

CHRISTIAN. Therefore thou never hadst one good thought concerning thyself in thy life. But let me go on. As the Word passeth a judgment upon our heart, so it passeth a judgment upon our ways; and when our thoughts of our hearts and ways agree with the judgment which the Word giveth of both, then are both good, because agreeing thereto.

IGNORANCE. Make out your meaning.

CHRISTIAN. Why, the Word of God saith that man's ways are crooked ways; not good, but perverse.[222] It saith they are naturally out of the good way, that they have not known it (Rom. 3). Now, when a man thus thinketh of his ways; I say, when he doth sensibly, and with heart humiliation, thus think, then hath he good thoughts of his own ways, because his thoughts now agree with the judgment of the Word of God.

IGNORANCE. What are good thoughts concerning God?

CHRISTIAN. Even as I have said concerning ourselves, when our thoughts of God do agree with what the Word saith of Him; and that is, when we think of His being and attributes as the Word hath taught, of which I cannot now discourse at large; but to speak of Him with reference to us: Then we have right thoughts of God, when we think that He knows us better than we know ourselves, and can see sin in us when and where we can see none in ourselves; when we think He knows our inmost thoughts, and that our heart, with all its depths, is always open unto His eyes; also, when we think that all our righteousness stinks in His nostrils, and

222 Psa. 125; Prov. 2:15

that, therefore, He cannot abide to see us stand before Him in any confidence, even in all our best performances.

IGNORANCE. Do you think that I am such a fool as to think God can see no further than I? or, that I would come to God in the best of my performances?

CHRISTIAN. Why, how dost thou think in this matter?

IGNORANCE. Why, to be short, I think I must believe in Christ for justification.

CHRISTIAN. How! think thou must believe in Christ, when thou seest not thy need of Him! Thou neither seest thy original nor actual infirmities; but hast such an opinion of thyself, and of what thou dost, as plainly renders thee to be one that did never see a necessity of Christ's personal righteousness to justify thee before God. How, then, dost thou say, I believe in Christ?

IGNORANCE. I believe well enough for all that.

CHRISTIAN. How dost thou believe?

IGNORANCE. I believe that Christ died for sinners; and that I shall be justified before God from the curse, through His gracious acceptance of my obedience to His law. Or thus, Christ makes my duties, that are religious, acceptable to His Father, by virtue of His merits; and so shall I be justified.

CHRISTIAN. Let me give an answer to this confession of thy faith.

1. Thou believest with a fantastical faith; for this faith is nowhere described in the Word.

2. Thou believest with a false faith; because it taketh justification from the personal righteousness of Christ, and applies it to thy own.

3. This faith maketh not Christ a justifier of thy person, but of thy actions; and of thy person for thy actions' sake, which is false.

4. Therefore, this faith is deceitful, even such as will

leave thee under wrath, in the day of God Almighty; for true justifying faith puts the soul, as sensible of its lost condition by the law, upon flying for refuge unto Christ's righteousness, which righteousness of His is not an act of grace, by which He maketh, for justification, thy obedience accepted with God; but His personal obedience to the law, in doing and suffering for us what that required at our hands; this righteousness, I say, true faith accepteth; under the skirt of which, the soul being shrouded, and by it presented as spotless before God, it is accepted, and acquit from condemnation.

IGNORANCE. What! would you have us trust to what Christ, in His own person, has done without us? This conceit would loosen the reins of our lust, and tolerate us to live as we list; for what matter how we live, if we may be justified by Christ's personal righteousness from all, when we believe it?

CHRISTIAN. Ignorance is thy name, and as thy name is, so art thou; even this thy answer demonstrateth what I say. Ignorant thou art of what justifying righteousness is, and as ignorant how to secure thy soul, through the faith of it, from the heavy wrath of God. Yea, thou also art ignorant of the true effects of saving faith in this righteousness of Christ, which is, to bow and win over the heart to God in Christ, to love His name, His Word, ways, and people, and not as thou ignorantly imaginest.

HOPEFUL. Ask him if ever he had Christ revealed to him from Heaven.

IGNORANCE. What! you are a man for revelations! I believe that what both you, and all the rest of you, say about that matter, is but the fruit of distracted brains.

HOPEFUL. Why, man! Christ is so hid in God from the natural apprehensions of the flesh, that He cannot by any man be savingly known, unless God the Father reveals Him to them.

IGNORANCE. That is your faith, but not mine; yet mine, I doubt not, is as good as yours, though I have not in my head so many whimsies as you.

CHRISTIAN. Give me leave to put in a word. You ought not so slightly to speak of this matter; for this I will boldly affirm, even as my good companion hath done, that no man can know Jesus Christ but by the revelation of the Father;[223] yea, and faith too, by which the soul layeth hold upon Christ, if it be right, must be wrought by the exceeding greatness of His mighty power; the working of which faith, I perceive, poor Ignorance, thou art ignorant of.[224] Be awakened then, see thine own wretchedness, and fly to the Lord Jesus; and by His righteousness, which is the righteousness of God, for He Himself is God, thou shalt be delivered from condemnation.

IGNORANCE. You go so fast, I cannot keep pace with you. Do you go on before; I must stay a while behind.

Then they said—

Well, Ignorance, wilt thou yet foolish be,
To slight good counsel, ten times given thee?
And if thou yet refuse it, thou shalt know,
Ere long, the evil of thy doing so.
Remember, man, in time, stoop, do not fear;
Good counsel taken well, saves: therefore hear.
But if thou yet shalt slight it, thou wilt be
The loser (Ignorance) I'll warrant thee.

Then Christian addressed thus himself to his fellow—

223 Matt. 11:27
224 1 Cor. 12:3; Eph 1:18, 19

CHRISTIAN. Well, come, my good Hopeful, I perceive that thou and I must walk by ourselves again.

So I saw in my dream that they went on apace before, and Ignorance he came bobbling after. Then said Christian to his companion, It pities me much for this poor man, it will certainly go ill with him at last.

HOPEFUL. Alas! there are abundance in our town in his condition, whole families, yea, whole streets, and that of pilgrims too; and if there be so many in our parts, how many, think you, must there be in the place where he was born?

CHRISTIAN. Indeed the Word saith, "He hath blinded their eyes, lest they should see," etc. But now we are by ourselves, what do you think of such men? Have they at no time, think you, convictions of sin, and so consequently fears that their state is dangerous?

HOPEFUL. Nay, do you answer that question yourself, for you are the elder man.

CHRISTIAN. Then I say, sometimes (as I think) they may; but they being naturally ignorant, understand not that such convictions tend to their good; and therefore they do desperately seek to stifle them, and presumptuously continue to flatter themselves in the way of their own hearts.

HOPEFUL. I do believe, as you say, that fear tends much to men's good, and to make them right, at their beginning to go on pilgrimage.

CHRISTIAN. Without all doubt it doth, if it be right; for so says the Word, "The fear of the Lord is the beginning of wisdom".[225]

HOPEFUL. How will you describe right fear?

CHRISTIAN. True or right fear is discovered by three things—

1. By its rise; it is caused by saving convictions for sin.

225 Prov. 1:7; 9:10; Psa. 111:10; Job. 28:28

2. It driveth the soul to lay fast hold of Christ for salvation.

3. It begetteth and continueth in the soul a great reverence of God, his Word, and ways, keeping it tender, and making it afraid to turn from them, to the right hand or to the left, to anything, that may dishonour God, break its peace, grieve the Spirit, or cause the enemy to speak reproachfully.

HOPEFUL. Well said; I believe you have said the truth. Are we now almost got past the Enchanted Ground?

CHRISTIAN. Why, art thou weary of this discourse?

HOPEFUL. No, verily, but that I would know where we are.

CHRISTIAN. We have not now above two miles further to go thereon. But let us return to our matter. Now the ignorant know not that such convictions as tend to put them in fear are for their good, and therefore they seek to stifle them.

HOPEFUL. How do they seek to stifle them?

CHRISTIAN. 1. They think that those fears are wrought by the devil (though indeed they are wrought of God); and, thinking so, they resist them as things that directly tend to their overthrow. 2. They also think that these fears tend to the spoiling of their faith, when, alas for them, poor men that they are, they have none at all! and therefore they harden their hearts against them. 3. They presume they ought not to fear; and therefore, in despite of them, wax presumptuously confident. 4. They see that those fears tend to take away from them their pitiful old self-holiness, and therefore they resist them with all their might.

HOPEFUL. I know something of this myself; for, before I knew myself, it was so with me.

CHRISTIAN. Well, we will leave, at this time, our neighbour Ignorance by himself, and fall upon another profitable question.

HOPEFUL. With all my heart, but you shall still begin.

CHRISTIAN. Well then, did you not know, about 10 years ago, one Temporary in your parts, who was a forward man in religion then?

HOPEFUL. Know him! yes, he dwelt in Graceless, a town about two miles off of Honesty, and he dwelt next door to one Turnback.

CHRISTIAN. Right, he dwelt under the same roof with him. Well, that man was much awakened once; I believe that then he had some sight of his sins, and of the wages that were due thereto.

HOPEFUL. I am of your mind, for, my house not being above three miles from him, he would ofttimes come to me, and that with many tears. Truly I pitied the man, and was not altogether without hope of him; but one may see, it is not every one that cries, Lord, Lord.

CHRISTIAN. He told me once that he was resolved to go on pilgrimage, as we do now; but all of a sudden he grew acquainted with one Save-self, and then he became a stranger to me.

HOPEFUL. Now, since we are talking about him, let us a little inquire into the reason of the sudden backsliding of him and such others.

CHRISTIAN. It may be very profitable, but do you begin.

HOPEFUL. Well then, there are in my judgment four reasons for it—

1. Though the consciences of such men are awakened, yet their minds are not changed; therefore, when the power of guilt weareth away, that which provoked them to be religious ceaseth, wherefore they naturally turn to their own course again, even as we see the dog that is sick of what he has eaten, so long as his sickness prevails, he vomits and casts up all; not that he doth this of a free mind (if we may say a dog has a mind), but because it troubleth his stomach; but

now, when his sickness is over, and so his stomach eased, his desire being not at all alienate from his vomit, he turns him about and licks up all, and so it is true which is written, "The dog is turned to his own vomit again".[226] Thus I say, being hot for Heaven, by virtue only of the sense and fear of the torments of hell, as their sense of hell, and the fears of damnation, chills and cools, so their desires for Heaven and salvation cool also. So then it comes to pass, that when their guilt and fear is gone, their desires for Heaven and happiness die, and they return to their course again.

2. Another reason is, they have slavish fears that do overmaster them; I speak now of the fears that they have of men, for "the fear of man bringeth a snare".[227] So then, though they seem to be hot for Heaven, so long as the flames of hell are about their ears, yet, when that terror is a little over, they betake themselves to second thoughts; namely, that it is good to be wise, and not to run (for they know not what) the hazard of losing all, or, at least, of bringing themselves into unavoidable and unnecessary troubles, and so they fall in with the world again.

3. The shame that attends religion lies also as a block in their way; they are proud and haughty, and religion in their eye is low and contemptible; therefore, when they have lost their sense of hell and wrath to come, they return again to their former course.

4. Guilt, and to meditate terror, are grievous to them. They like not to see their misery before they come into it; though perhaps the sight of it first, if they loved that sight, might make them fly whither the righteous fly and are safe. But because they do, as I hinted before, even shun the thoughts of guilt and terror, therefore, when once they are

226 2 Peter 2:22

227 Prov. 29:25

rid of their awakenings about the terrors and wrath of God, they harden their hearts gladly, and choose such ways as will harden them more and more.

CHRISTIAN. You are pretty near the business, for the bottom of all is, for want of a change in their mind and will. And therefore they are but like the felon that standeth before the judge, he quakes and trembles, and seems to repent most heartily, but the bottom of all is the fear of the halter; not that he hath any detestation of the offence, as is evident, because, let but this man have his liberty, and he will be a thief, and so a rogue still, whereas, if his mind were changed, he would be otherwise.

HOPEFUL. Now, I have showed you the reasons of their going back, do you show me the manner thereof.

CHRISTIAN. So I will, willingly.

1. They draw off their thoughts, all that they may, from the remembrance of God, death, and judgment to come.

2. Then they cast off by degrees private duties, as closet prayer, curbing their lusts, watching, sorrow for sin, and the like.

3. Then they shun the company of lively and warm Christians.

4. After that, they grow cold to public duty, as hearing, reading, godly conference, and the like.

5. Then they begin to pick holes, as we say, in the coats of some of the godly; and that devilishly, that they may have a seeming colour to throw religion (for the sake of some infirmity they have espied in them) behind their backs.

6. Then they begin to adhere to, and associate themselves with, carnal, loose, and wanton men.

7. Then they give way to carnal and wanton discourses in secret; and glad are they if they can see such things in any that are counted honest, that they may the more boldly do it through their example.

8. After this, they begin to play with little sins openly.

9. And then, being hardened, they show themselves as they are. Thus, being launched again into the gulf of misery, unless a miracle of grace prevent it, they everlastingly perish in their own deceivings.

Now I saw in my dream, that by this time the Pilgrims were got over the Enchanted Ground, and entering into the country of Beulah, whose air was very sweet and pleasant, the way lying directly through it, they solaced themselves there for a season.[228] Yea, here they heard continually the singing of birds, and saw every day the flowers appear in the earth, and heard the voice of the turtle in the land.[229] In this country the sun shineth night and day; wherefore this was beyond the Valley of the Shadow of Death, and also out of the reach of Giant Despair, neither could they from this place so much as see Doubting Castle. Here they were within sight of the city they were going to, also here met them some of the inhabitants thereof; for in this land the Shining Ones commonly walked, because it was upon the borders of Heaven. In this land also the contract between the bride and the bridegroom was renewed; yea, here, "As the bridegroom rejoiceth over the bride, so did their God rejoice over them".[230] Here they had no want of corn and wine; for in this place they met with abundance of what they had sought for in all their pilgrimage.[231] Here they heard voices from out of the city, loud voices, saying, "Say ye to the daughter of Zion, Behold, thy salvation cometh! Behold, His reward is with Him!".[232] Here all the inhabitants of the country called

228 Isa. 62:4

229 Song. 2:10–12

230 Isa. 62:5

231 Isa. 62:8

232 Isa. 62:11

them, "The holy people, The redeemed of the Lord, Sought out," etc.[233]

Now, as they walked in this land, they had more rejoicing than in parts more remote from the kingdom to which they were bound; and drawing near to the city, they had yet a more perfect view thereof. It was builded of pearls and precious stones, also the street thereof was paved with gold; so that by reason of the natural glory of the city, and the reflection of the sunbeams upon it, Christian with desire fell sick. Hopeful also had a fit or two of the same disease. Wherefore, here they lay by it a while, crying out, because of their pangs, "If ye find my Beloved, tell Him that I am sick of love.[234]

But being a little strengthened, and better able to bear their sickness, they walked on their way, and came yet nearer and nearer, where were orchards, vineyards, and gardens, and their gates opened into the highway. Now, as they came up to these places, behold, the gardener stood in the way, to whom the Pilgrims said, Whose goodly vineyards and gardens are these? He answered, They are the King's, and are planted here for His own delight, and also for the solace of pilgrims. So the gardener had them into the vineyards, and bid them refresh themselves with the dainties.[235] He also showed them there the King's walks, and the arbours, where He delighted to be; and here they tarried and slept.

Now I beheld in my dream, that they talked more in their sleep at this time than ever they did in all their journey; and being in a muse thereabout, the gardener said even to me, Wherefore musest thou at the matter? It is the nature

233 Isa. 62:12

234 Song. 5:8

235 Deut. 23:24

of the fruit of the grapes of these vineyards to go down so sweetly, as to cause the lips of them that are asleep to speak.

So I saw that when they awoke, they addressed themselves to go up to the city. But, as I said, the reflection of the sun upon the city (for "the city was pure gold"),[236] was so extremely glorious, that they could not, as yet, with open face behold it, but through an instrument made for that purpose (2 Cor. v). So I saw, that as they went on, there met them two men, in raiment that shone like gold; also their faces shone as the light.

These men asked the Pilgrims whence they came; and they told them. They also asked them where they had lodged, what difficulties and dangers, what comforts and pleasures they had met in the way; and they told them. Then said the men that met them, You have but two difficulties more to meet with, and then you are in the city.

Christian then, and his companion, asked the men to go along with them; so they told them they would. But, said they, you must obtain it by your own faith. So I saw in my dream that they went on together, until they came in sight of the gate.

Now, I further saw, that betwixt them and the gate was a river, but there was no bridge to go over; the river was very deep. At the sight, therefore, of this river, the Pilgrims were much stunned: but the men that went with them said, You must go through, or you cannot come at the gate.

The Pilgrims then began to inquire if there was no other way to the gate; to which they answered, Yes; but there hath not any, save two, to wit, Enoch and Elijah, been permitted to tread that path, since the foundation of the world, nor shall, until the last trumpet shall sound).[237] The Pilgrims

236 Rev. 21:18

237 1 Cor. 15:51, 52

then, especially Christian, began to despond in their minds, and looked this way and that, but no way could be found by them, by which they might escape the river. Then they asked the men if the waters were all of a depth. They said, No; yet they could not help them in that case; for, said they, you shall find it deeper or shallower, as you believe in the King of the place.

They then addressed themselves to the water; and entering, Christian began to sink, and crying out to his good friend Hopeful, he said, I sink in deep waters; the billows go over my head, all his waves go over me! Selah.

Then said the other, Be of good cheer, my brother, I feel the bottom, and it is good. Then, said Christian, Ah! my friend, "the sorrows of death have compassed me about"; I shall not see the land that flows with milk and honey; and with that a great darkness and horror fell upon Christian, so that he could not see before him. Also here he in great measure lost his senses, so that he could neither remember, nor orderly talk of any of those sweet refreshments that he had met with in the way of his pilgrimage. But all the words that he spake still tended to discover that he had horror of mind, and heart fears that he should die in that river, and never obtain entrance in at the gate. Here also, as they that stood by perceived, he was much in the troublesome thoughts of the sins that he had committed, both since and before he began to be a pilgrim. It was also observed that he was troubled with apparitions of hobgoblins and evil spirits; for ever and anon he would intimate so much by words. Hopeful, therefore, here had much ado to keep his brother's head above water; yea, sometimes he would be quite gone down, and then, ere awhile, he would rise up again half dead. Hopeful also would endeavour to comfort him, saying, Brother, I see the gate, and men standing by to receive us; but Christian would answer, It is you, it is you they wait for; you have been Hopeful ever since I knew you. And so have you, said he to Christian. Ah, brother! said he, surely if I were right He would now arise to help me; but for my sins He hath brought me into the snare, and hath left me. Then said Hopeful, My brother, you have quite forgot the text, where it is said of the wicked, "There are no bands in their death; but their strength is firm. They are not in trouble as other men, neither are they plagued like other men.[238] These troubles and distresses that you go through in these waters are no sign that God hath forsaken you; but are sent to try you, whether you will call to mind that which heretofore you have received of His goodness, and live upon Him in your distresses. Then I saw in my dream, that Christian was as in a muse a while. To whom also Hopeful added this word, Be of good cheer, Jesus Christ maketh thee whole; and with that Christian brake out with a loud voice, O! I see Him again, and He tells me, "When thou passest through the waters, I will be with thee; and through the rivers, they shall not overflow thee".[239] Then they both took courage, and the enemy was after that as still as a stone, until they were gone over. Christian therefore presently found ground to stand upon, and so it followed that the rest of the river was but shallow. Thus they got over. Now, upon the bank of the river, on the other side, they saw the two shining men again, who there waited for them; wherefore, being come out of the river, they saluted them, saying, We are ministering spirits, sent forth to minister for those that shall be heirs of salvation. Thus they went along towards the gate. Now you must note that the city stood upon a mighty hill, but the Pilgrims went up that hill with ease, because they had these two men to lead them up by the arms; also, they had left their mortal

238 Psa. 73:4, 5

239 Isa. 43:2

garments behind them in the river, for though they went in with them, they came out without them. They, therefore, went up here with much agility and speed, though the foundation upon which the city was framed was higher than the clouds. They, therefore, went up through the regions of the air, sweetly talking as they went, being comforted, because they safely got over the river, and had such glorious companions to attend them.

The talk they had with the Shining Ones was about the glory of the place; who told them that the beauty and glory of it was inexpressible. There, said they, is the "Mount Zion, the heavenly Jerusalem, the innumerable company of angels, and the spirits of just men made perfect".[240] You are going now, said they, to the paradise of God, wherein you shall see the tree of life, and eat of the never-fading fruits thereof; and when you come there, you shall have white robes given you, and your walk and talk shall be every day with the King, even all the days of eternity.[241] There you shall not see again such things as you saw when you were in the lower region upon the earth, to wit, sorrow, sickness, affliction, and death, "for the former things are passed away." You are now going to Abraham, to Isaac, and Jacob, and to the prophets—men that God hath taken away from the evil to come, and that are now resting upon their beds, each one walking in his righteousness.[242] The men then asked, what must we do in the holy place? To whom it was answered, You must there receive the comforts of all your toil, and have joy for all your sorrow; you must reap what you have sown, even the fruit of all your prayers, and tears, and suffer-

240 Heb. 12:22–24

241 Rev. 2:7; 3:4; 22:5

242 Isa. 57:1, 2; 65:17

ings for the King by the way.[243] In that place you must wear crowns of gold, and enjoy the perpetual sight and vision of the Holy One, for "there you shall see Him as He is".[244] There also you shall serve Him continually with praise, with shouting and thanksgiving, whom you desired to serve in the world, though with much difficulty, because of the infirmity of your flesh. There your eyes shall be delighted with seeing, and your ears with hearing the pleasant voice of the Mighty One. There you shall enjoy your friends again, that are gone thither before you; and there you shall with joy receive, even every one that follows into the holy place after you. There also shall you be clothed with glory and majesty, and put into an equipage fit to ride out with the King of glory. When He shall come with sound of trumpet in the clouds, as upon the wings of the wind, you shall come with Him; and when He shall sit upon the throne of judgment, you shall sit by Him; yea, and when He shall pass sentence upon all the workers of iniquity, let them be angels or men, you also shall have a voice in that judgment, because they were His and your enemies.[245] Also when He shall again return to the city, you shall go too, with sound of trumpet, and be ever with Him.

243 Gal. 6:7

244 1 John 3:2

245 1 Thess. 4:13–17; Jude 14; Dan. 7:9, 10; 1 Cor. 6:2, 3

MINISTERING SPIRITS MEET CHRISTIAN AND HOPEFUL

Now, while they were thus drawing towards the gate, behold a company of the heavenly host came out to meet them; to whom it was said, by the other two Shining Ones, These are the men that have loved our Lord when they were in the world, and that have left all for His holy name; and He hath sent us to fetch them, and we have brought them thus far on their desired journey, that they may go in and look their Redeemer in the face with joy. Then the heavenly host gave a great shout, saying, "Blessed are they which are called unto the marriage supper of the Lamb".[246] There came out also at this time to meet them, several of the King's trumpeters, clothed in white and shining raiment, who, with melodious noises, and loud, made even the heavens to echo with their sound. These trumpeters saluted Christian and his fellow with 10,000 welcomes from the world; and this they did with shouting, and sound of trumpet.

This done, they compassed them round on every side; some went before, some behind, and some on the right hand, some on the left (as it were to guard them through the upper regions), continually sounding as they went, with

246 Rev. 19:9

melodious noise, in notes on high; so that the very sight was to them that could behold it, as if Heaven itself was come down to meet them. Thus, therefore, they walked on together; and as they walked, ever and anon these trumpeters, even with joyful sound, would, by mixing their music with looks and gestures, still signify to Christian and his brother, how welcome they were into their company, and with what gladness they came to meet them; and now were these two men, as it were, in Heaven, before they came at it, being swallowed up with the sight of angels, and with hearing of their melodious notes. Here also they had the city itself in view, and they thought they heard all the bells therein to ring, to welcome them thereto. But above all, the warm and joyful thoughts that they had about their own dwelling there, with such company, and that forever and ever. O by what tongue or pen can their glorious joy be expressed! And thus they came up to the gate.

Now, when they were come up to the gate, there was written over it in letters of gold, "Blessed are they that do His commandments, that they may have right to the tree of life, and may enter in through the gates into the city".[247]

Then I saw in my dream, that the Shining Men bid them call at the gate; the which, when they did, some looked from above over the gate, to wit, Enoch, Moses, and Elijah, etc., to whom it was said, These pilgrims are come from the City of Destruction, for the love that they bear to the King of this place; and then the pilgrims gave in unto them each man his certificate, which they had received in the beginning; those, therefore, were carried into the King, who, when He had read them, said, Where are the men? To whom it was answered, They are standing without the gate. The King then

247 Rev. 22:14

commanded to open the gate, "That the righteous nation," said He, "which keepeth the truth, may enter in".[248]

Now I saw in my dream that these two men went in at the gate; and lo, as they entered, they were transfigured, and they had raiment put on that shone like gold. There were also that met them with harps and crowns, and gave them to them—the harps to praise withal, and the crowns in token of honour. Then I heard in my dream that all the bells in the city rang again for joy, and that it was said unto them, "ENTER YE INTO THE JOY OF YOUR LORD." I also heard the men themselves, that they sang with a loud voice, saying, "BLESSING, AND HONOUR, AND GLORY, AND POWER, BE UNTO HIM THAT SITTETH UPON THE THRONE, AND UNTO THE LAMB, FOREVER AND EVER".[249]

Now just as the gates were opened to let in the men, I looked in after them, and, behold, the City shone like the sun; the streets also were paved with gold, and in them walked many men, with crowns on their heads, palms in their hands, and golden harps to sing praises withal. There were also of them that had wings, and they answered one another without intermission, saying, "Holy, holy, holy, is the Lord".[250] And after that, they shut up the gates; which, when I had seen, I wished myself among them.

Now while I was gazing upon all these things, I turned my head to look back, and saw Ignorance come up to the river side; but he soon got over, and that without half that difficulty which the other two men met with. For it happened that there was then in that place, one Vain-hope, a ferryman, that with his boat helped him over; so he, as the other I saw, did ascend the hill, to come up to the gate,

248 Isa. 26:2

249 Rev. 5:13

250 Rev. 4:8

only he came alone; neither did any man meet him with the least encouragement. When he was come up to the gate, he looked up to the writing that was above, and then began to knock, supposing that entrance should have been quickly administered to him; but he was asked by the men that looked over the top of the gate, Whence came you? and what would you have? He answered, I have eat and drank in the presence of the King, and He has taught in our streets. Then they asked him for his certificate, that they might go in and show it to the King; so he fumbled in his bosom for one, and found none. Then said they, Have you none? But the man answered never a word. So they told the King, but He would not come down to see him, but commanded the two Shining Ones that conducted Christian and Hopeful to the City, to go out and take Ignorance, and bind him hand and foot, and have him away. Then they took him up, and carried him through the air, to the door that I saw in the side of the hill, and put him in there. Then I saw that there was a way to hell, even from the gates of Heaven, as well as from the City of Destruction! So I awoke, and behold it was a dream.

THE CONCLUSION

Now, READER, I have told my dream to thee;
See if thou canst interpret it to me,
Or to thyself, or neighbour; but take heed
Of misinterpreting; for that, instead
Of doing good, will but thyself abuse:
By misinterpreting, evil ensues.
Take heed also, that thou be not extreme,
In playing with the outside of my dream:
Nor let my figure or similitude
Put thee into a laughter or a feud.
Leave this for boys and fools; but as for thee,
Do thou the substance of my matter see.
Put by the curtains, look within my veil,
Turn up my metaphors, and do not fail;
There, if thou seekest them, such things to find,
As will be helpful to an honest mind.
What of my dross thou findest there, be bold
To throw away, but yet preserve the gold;
What if my gold be wrapped up in ore?—
None throws away the apple for the core.
But if thou shalt cast all away as vain,
I know not but 'twill make me dream again.

THE END

SCRIPTURE INDEX

ACKNOWLEDGEMENTS

At the beginning of *The Pilgrim's Progress*, when Evangelist commissions Christian to "keep that light in your eye" and set out on the journey, Christian is described as running in tears, fingers in his ears, resisting the cries of his family, friends, and foes who might convince him to stay. This initial lack of support in Christian's story is envied by no one—and nothing could be further from the truth in the events that surrounded our efforts to tell his story afresh.

Since the team at *desiringGod.org* first entertained the idea of publishing a new version of Bunyan's classic, there emerged a sweet fellowship for the road that lay ahead, and I would be amiss not to make mention of my companions now by way of thanks to God and them. Thank you, David Mathis, for your executive leadership and unremitting loyalty to produce good content. Thank you, Marshall Segal, for your attention to my questions and the whimsical suggestion to publish John Piper's biography not simultaneous to this present volume, but within it. Thank you, Stefan Green, for your encouraging optimism about us trying new things in content production and resource development. Thank you, Tony Reinke, for your research skills, and appreciation for the man, John Newton. His 1776 preface gives this version a special touch, and that is owing to you, both in your discovery of the preface at the Library of Congress and your generosity to let us include it.

Special thanks along the way also goes to Leland Ryken, who served as a consultant on this project from the beginning and offered wonderful advice along the way. Thank you, Caleb Kormann, our summer intern, for doing the meticulous work of reformatting the text and rearranging Scripture citations in order to increase readability. Also, thank you, Peter Voth and Ryan Leichty, for your artistic skill in the cover and typesetting, respectively.

Thank you, John Piper, for your great service to the saints in telling the lives of past saints, in particular your biography of John Bunyan that encourages us, especially in the midst of suffering, to live upon God and his word. Our hope is that this new edition of *The Pilgrim's Progress* might be one small means to help us on our way.

"For here we have no lasting city, but we seek the city that is to come" (Heb. 13:14).

Jonathan Parnell
desiringGod.org

ACKNOWLEDGEMENTS

desiringGod

Everyone wants to be happy. Our website was born and built for happiness. We want people everywhere to understand and embrace the truth that God is most glorified in us when we are most satisfied in him. We've collected more than thirty years of John Piper's speaking and writing, including translations into more than forty languages. We also provide a daily stream of new written, audio, and video resources to help you find truth, purpose, and satisfaction that never end. And it's all available free of charge, thanks to the generosity of people who've been blessed by the ministry.

If you want more resources for true happiness, or if you want to learn more about our work at Desiring God, we invite you to visit us at www.desiringGod.org.

www.desiringGod.org

Made in the USA
Columbia, SC
24 April 2019